First-Line Management

First-Line Management:
The Foreman's Role in Manufacturing

Ivan R. Vernon, Editor

Authors

In organizing, developing, and writing this book, the co-authors listed below have generously donated their time, effort, and professional skills in order to contribute to the advancement of manufacturing management.

Dr. Chester L. Brisley, Director
Engineering Center for Postgraduate and
    Professional Development
The University of Wisconsin—Milwaukee

Edward F. Dolan, Director
Manufacturing Engineering Service
Allis-Chalmers Manufacturing Company

Louis E. Jenkins,
Manager of Training
South Bend Divisions
The Bendix Corporation

Henry L. Kaminski, Manager
Manufacturing Engineering
Brake & Steering Division
The Bendix Corporation

Dr. Donald L. Kirkpatrick,
Professor of Management Development
The University of Wisconsin—Milwaukee

Roger Locher,
Assistant Superintendent
Buick Motor Division
General Motors Corporation

George H. Morgan,
New Products Engineer
Auto Specialties Manufacturing Company

Irvin Otis, Chief Industrial Engineer
Kaiser Jeep Division
American Motors Corporation

Joseph R. Ryan, Principal
A. T. Kearney & Company, Inc.
Chicago, Illinois

Published by:
Society of Manufacturing Engineers
Dearborn, Michigan
1972

Manufacturing Management Series

First-Line Management

Copyright © 1972 by the
Society of Manufacturing Engineers,
Dearborn, Michigan   48128.
First Edition

Library of Congress Catalog Card Number: 70-144105
International Standard Book Number: 0-87263-028-5.

MANUFACTURED IN THE UNITED STATES OF AMERICA

Preface

More and more companies today are realizing the importance of first-line management. Less and less is the foreman today's "forgotten man of management." Nevertheless, inadequate approaches are often used in developing an effective first-line management team. Too often the foreman is overlooked when management training programs are designed, when compensation systems are established, and when promotions are considered.

First-Line Management provides an overview of the foreman's function and role in American industry. Directed to foremen and higher management, this book offers numerous helpful suggestions for first-line supervisors and describes for higher management the aspects of the foreman's function. Its purpose is to answer some of the perplexing questions frequently asked about first-line management. The authors are men with many years of experience in manufacturing management. Their experience should serve you well as you begin thinking of ways in which to improve the performance of foremen in your organization, or as you, as a foreman, start coming to grips with management problems.

This book represents the cooperative effort of numerous individuals. The outline was prepared by the First-Line Management Subdivision of SME's Manufacturing Management Division. Members of the Subdivision, working with the editor, then successively refined the outline, and then either accepted writing responsibilities or recommended authors whom they felt were well qualified. The members of the Subdivision include the Chairman, Donald H. Major, The Bendix Corporation; Dr. Chester L. Brisley, Director of the Engineering Center for Postgraduate and Professional Development of the University Extension of the University of Wisconsin; Edward F. Dolan, Allis-Chalmers Manufacturing Company; Dr. Donald Kirkpatrick, Professor of Management Development, University Extension, The University of Wisconsin; Roger Locher, General Motors Corporation; George H. Morgan, Auto Specialties Manufacturing Company; Irvin Otis, American Motors Jeep Corporation; Joseph R. Ryan, A. T. Kearney & Company, Inc.; D. W. Laycock, The Bendix Corporation; and E. T. Gleason, Marathon Oil Company. The composition of the Divisions and Subdivisions of the Society's Technical Division structure changes from time to time, and this listing is intended only to acknowledge the contribution of the individuals who were most concerned with the planning for this book.

The Authors

The authors, all of whom are members of the Subdivision, are listed on the title page. As with past volumes in the Manufacturing Management Series, the authors are not identified with the individual chapters for which they were primarily responsible. The reason for this is that each author contributed more to the book than the specific chapter that he wrote. The authors individually and collectively prepared chapter outlines, reviewed and revised them. When they completed the writing of their own chapters, they then reviewed the manuscripts for all of the other chapters and provided suggestions to the other writers. The purpose of this participative process was to produce an integrated text which would be more than a collection of several points of view.

Nevertheless, it is desirable to recognize the primary authors of each chapter. Chapter 1 was written by Edward F. Dolan, Chapter 2 by Louis E. Jenkins, and Chapter 3 by Henry L. Kaminski. Chapter 4 was authored by Joseph R. Ryan, Chapter 5 by Roger Locher, Chapter 6 by Dr. Donald R. Kirkpatrick, Chapter 7 by Irvin Otis, and Chapter 8 by Dr. Chester L. Brisley. While George Morgan did not have responsibility for any one chapter, he provided valuable service by reviewing chapter outlines and writing extensive passages which the various authors incorporated into the individual chapters. Donald Major first proposed this book and was the coordinator of the efforts of the various authors.

As explained on the title page, each of these authors participated in the preparation of this book without compensation. The Society of Manufacturing Engineers expresses its sincere appreciation to these authors for their contributions to the advancement of manufacturing management.

November 15, 1971   Ivan R. Vernon
Kent, Ohio

Contents

First-Line Management

Chapter 1

The Scope of Foremanship

What is a foreman? What does he do? What are some of the problems that foremen face? These are the types of questions discussed in this chapter. First we will examine some of the generally accepted definitions in this area, and see how well they relate to current situations. Next we will discuss the role of the foreman in order to arrive at a clear concept of his contribution to the manufacturing enterprise. Finally, we will describe some of the most pressing problems that are currently facing today's foreman.

SOME DEFINITIONS

The term *foreman* is used widely throughout industry to describe a particular type of leadership position. Unfortunately, the term does not have the same meaning, or connotation, in all plants or in all industries, nor does it always imply the same degree of responsibility. Generally speaking, the term refers to anyone with leadership responsibilities, in a position to direct the efforts of other people, with continuing personal contact with the work force on the one hand, and with company management on the other. To the hourly worker in the shop—the rank-and-file employee—the foreman is the first line of management. He is the visible, everyday, representative of the authority of management.

In addition to the title of *foreman,* there are numerous other terms applied to this position: *boss, chief, group leader, lead man, overseer, taskmaster, superintendent, captain, supervisor,* and many others. In recent years, as the foreman's job has become more complex, and as top management has come to realize the importance of the position, the term *supervisor* has begun to replace the term *foreman.* In the succeeding chapters of this book, the terms *foreman, supervisor,* and *first-line manager* are used interchangeably.

By way of introduction, we will examine the currently accepted definitions of these terms. For example, Webster defines the terms *foreman* and *supervision* as follows:

> *Foreman:* A first or chief man . . . a member of a jury who acts as chairman and spokesman . . . a chief and often specially trained workman who works with and commonly leads a gang or crew . . . a person in authority over a group of workers, a particular operation, or a section of a plant.

3

Supervision: To oversee for direction; to superintend; to inspect with authority; to exercise supervision. (From the Latin "super" meaning "over" and "videre" meaning "to see".)[1]

In addition to these academic definitions many others have been offered. Two of the more recent efforts at defining the foreman's job include the following:

Our foremen are part of management. They have been called the "cutting edge" of the management tool . . . they translate management plans, objectives, and programs into actual accomplishments.[2]

Foremanship is the process of implementing management's planning and direction by organizing a work group and a work plan to achieve management's objectives.[3]

In this chapter we do not attempt to describe in detail all aspects of the foreman's job, but we do list his major responsibilities. This is necessary in order to indicate what the foreman's job includes and to define the terms we will be using. We can think of the foreman's job as consisting of three major functions: planning, directing, and controlling. Obviously, the foreman must first develop a plan which will guide him in the effective use of his men, materials, and machines. He is aided by various staff departments in developing plans to accomplish the work of his department. His second responsibility, directing, is concerned with the important task of overseeing his personnel as they perform the work assigned to them. His third responsibility, controlling, is concerned with the checking—or follow-up—of men, materials, and machines to assure that schedules are met and plans are accomplished.

In performing these three functions, a foreman sometimes acts as a supervisor and sometimes as a manager. Much of what a foreman does during the ordinary working day is supervisory in nature. Overseeing his group, reporting production counts, checking quality levels, noting the condition of facilities, and training his people—these are all elements of the supervisory portion of this job. But when the foreman translates his superintendent's plan into his own group plan, when he initiates correction of production bottlenecks, when he factors in improved methods, and when he anticipates difficulties, then he is acting as a manager, or *foreman/manager.*

To understand more precisely what is meant by the term *foreman/manager,* or first-line manager, we will need to review briefly the relationships of the various levels of management to each other. When the factory system of manufacturing was established, a concept of management emerged which has resulted in the development of a highly productive economy. Management has come to be recognized as a discipline that achieves established objectives by emphasizing the most efficient utilization of human efforts and resources. In the application of this management concept, terms such as *top management, middle management,* and *supervisory management,* have become commonly used. Often, there is no clear definition of these terms, and the meanings attached to them will differ from one company to another. To aid in differentiating between these three levels of management, the following classification has been adopted by the executive compensation service of the American Management Association:

Top Management . . . This is the policy-making group responsible for the overall direction and success of all company activities. It is made up of the Board Chairman, President, Directors

---

1. *Webster's Third New International Dictionary*
2. Glenn Gardiner, *Foremen in Action* (Elliott, 1960).
3. Frank A. Busse, *Three-Dimensional Foremanship* (AMA, 1969).

who are also officers, other officers, and key top management personnel. Positions other than the Chairman, President, and often Executive Vice-President, or General Manager, are usually directly responsible for a major division or function of the business, but each also carries a responsibility for the performance of the business as a whole, participating in decisions of a company-wide nature and collaborating with others in the group in important matters affecting any or all phases of the company's operation.

Middle Management . . . This group is responsible for the execution and interpretation of policies throughout the organization and for the successful operation of assigned divisions or departments. They have a high degree of responsibility for individual initiative and judgement, acting under policies and directives of top management. They have the responsibility for recommending new or revised policies and for establishing objectives of their assigned activities. They usually accomplish results through lower levels of supervision. Important staff functions may be assigned to this group.

Supervisory Management . . . This is the supervision directly responsible to the Middle Management group for final execution of policies by the rank and file employees, and for attainment of objectives in assigned organizational units through practices and procedures approved and issued by Top or Middle Management. It may include assistants to middle management positions and staff functions of a lesser nature than those in the the two upper management groups.[4]

It has always been recognized that first line supervisors perform a vital management function, but their status has not been clear. Contributing to this uncertainty of status has been the controversy over whether supervisors should be allowed to join unions or to form their own unions, an uncertainty about the extent of their authority, and the question as to whether they are really part of the management team. Other problems include the many petty tasks with which foremen have been saddled, their exclusion from management development programs, and the shortcomings in their selection and training. In well-managed companies serious attempts are being made to improve the supervisor's status and to include him in management activities. Some of the prerogatives that have been removed from the supervisor's job have been restored to bring the status of the position more in line with his responsibilities.

The past ten years have brought improvement in methods of training supervisors, as well as in management's concept of the nature of the supervisor's job. The current trend is to select the supervisor on the basis of leadership and management ability, rather than for superior performance as a technician, mechanic, or production worker. The tendency is also to delegate to him more authority in personnel selection and merit rating. Development programs are now concentrating on performance-centered training, and are increasing the supervisor's decision-making ability and communication skills.

What are the supervisory skills that help us appraise a potential foreman's fitness to lead a work group? There are a number of skills that could be listed, depending upon who is asked the question and what industry is involved. However, the experience of others in the past suggests that the following five factors are good indicators[5]:

1) Ability to organize the activities of others
2) Insight into human behavior, both one's own and that of others
3) Leadership or dominance in face-to-face situations
4) The emotional control of self and others, and ability to maintain steady output without emotional stress under trying and varying circumstances

---

4. Carl Heyel, *The Encyclopedia of Management* (Reinhold, 1963), 476.

5. C. D. Flory and J. E. Janney, "Psychological Services to Business Leaders," *Journal of Consulting Psychology,* Vol. 10 (1946), 15–19.

5) Practical decision making, which demonstrates ability to perceive significant factors and evaluate the relative importance of goals based on intelligent, well-seasoned risk taking.

The subject of supervision and leadership skills is broad, encompassing such items as morale, discipline, training, management types, attitudes, human relations, communications, and sensitivity. The essential point for the foreman to remember is this: He will succeed in his job according to how well he is able to secure results from the people he supervises. Technical proficiency can assist him in his performance as a supervisor in only a secondary manner. While a man can be promoted to foreman because of his technical knowledge, he will stand or fall as a foreman on the strength of how well he is able to handle the people under him.

We have said that there are a number of points of difference between the top, middle, and supervisory levels of management. Primary among these differences is the fact that the foreman, or first-line supervisor, is responsible for the final execution of the policies and directives of management. He is the final interface between the factory employee and plant management. It is the foreman's interpretation of management's directives that is passed on to the worker.

We can see that the main point of distinction between the foreman and higher levels of management is in the supervision of operating personnel. In the manufacturing organization, in general, the foreman is the only manager who does not supervise other managers. The foreman represents the first line of management to the rank and file employees. In this role, the foreman is often the only member of the management team with which the workers come in contact. Certainly he is the only management representative they see with any regularity.

THE ROLE OF THE FOREMAN—AN HISTORICAL VIEW

There have been many changes in the role of the foreman over the past 100 years. These changes have been very dramatic and are still in process. They are principally the result of our shifting patterns of work and production. For centuries people have worked—either individually or collectively—to produce goods and services. In primitive times, the production of goods consisted of the elemental processes involved in the preparation of food, shelter, clothing, weapons, and tools—usually for the consumption or use of the individual or his family. This "manufacturing" in the home, of products intended solely for domestic consumption, was the customary early pattern.

It is probable that the first advance in this earliest manufacturing practice resulted from the specialization of labor. Some member of a household was able to produce a surplus of food, clothing, shelter, tools, or other commodities which could be bartered outside for some other product or service. Whether the group producing these items consisted of one family or group of families, it is probable that the members assumed jobs in accordance with their skills. Probably some particularly respected member of the group acted to allocate tasks and represent them to other groups. This specialization of labor was a major milestone in man's progress towards civilization.

History is replete with examples of this kind of work arrangement. As the agricultural economy gave way to the development of towns and cities, specialization of talents and skills increased. Workers with well-developed skills in building, weaving, metalworking, or other handicrafts were able to devote all of their energies to their field of specialty. Thus it was that numerous trades, such as those of the carpenter, wheelwright, coppersmith, weaver, tanner, and baker, came into being. In time, it was inevitable that these expert workers would decide to combine for mutual benefit and protection according to their distinctive handicrafts. Thus, in the Middle Ages, such combinations gradually became quite powerful and were able to exercise control over individual members and their products.[6] In Europe these craft-type organizations became known as guilds. These guilds can be considered the forerunner of today's labor unions. The members of these guilds selected one of their group to "go to the fore" to represent them in discussions and negotiations with their masters and with other guilds. In fulfilling this leadership or representative role, the person selected became known as a foreman.

In the early eighteenth century, throughout most of Europe and the new American colonies, farming was still the major occupation. The average man was a farmer living in or near a village, raising his own food, and producing clothing, furniture, and tools at home from materials produced on his farm. In the towns, which were generally small, some manufacturing was conducted. Hardware, cloth, jewelry, swords, and guns were produced by craftsmen working in their own shops with relatively simple tools. Products manufactured in the towns were exchanged for food produced in the farming districts. Items manufactured in Europe were also exported overseas in payment for luxuries imported from abroad, or were sold to the colonies to pay for materials which the colonists sent to Europe. On the whole, the picture of European life before 1750 is that of a sparse population, primarily agrarian, hungry much of the time, diseased, and living at a low fixed standard.[7]

This picture changed greatly in England in about 1750 with great increases in both agricultural and industrial production. These changes were brought about largely by a series of epic-making inventions. These inventions, primarily in the textile and iron-making industries, permitted greatly increased volumes of production. The invention of the spinning jenny and the power weaving loom provided a tremendous boost in productivity to the English textile industry. Similarly, the invention of the steam engine and the invention of the grooved rolling mill provided a similar stimulus to the iron-making industry. The effects of the Industrial Revolution are, of course, history and are well documented. Although the costs of machinery, and the costs of buildings to house this machinery, required a far greater outlay of capital than was necessary to provide the simple hand tools used by craftsmen, costs of production were so greatly reduced by this method that the development of the factory system of manufacturing was inevitable.

The Industrial Revolution in the United States did not begin at the same time as that in England. Although there were numerous inventions and applications of new ideas in the textile field and in the iron industry during the late eighteenth and early nineteenth centuries, the Industrial Revolution in America did not really take root until the post-Civil War era. The coming of peace after the war introduced an era of industrial progress in which large-scale manufacturing developed rapidly. As a result the United States progressed steadily to reach the first rank among manufacturing nations—a position it still maintains a century later.

During the latter part of the nineteenth century and during the early years of the 1900s, the nation experienced a great expansion of employment. Mass production stimulated mass sales and kept industrial employment at a high level. It followed then that the large numbers of people working in industry necessitated increasing numbers of foremen

---

6. *The Lincoln Library of Essential Information* (The Frontier Press, 1924), 1345.
7. *The World Book Encyclopedia* (Field Enterprises, 1961), Vol. 9, 184.

to guide their activities. The foreman's role was primarily one of ensuring that the work assigned was accomplished in a timely manner. Physical size and strength were factors considered in his selection. He was usually chosen from the ranks primarily for his knowledge of the job and for his ability to get the work accomplished. He was not necessarily the best-liked man, nor perhaps even the most respected, but his responsibilities and authority were very clear.

To perhaps better compare the evolution of the role of the foreman, at least as we have known it in the United States, it might be well to consider the following excerpts from American literature:

Late Nineteenth Century:

> I am an American. I was born and reared in Hartford, in the state of Connecticut—anyway, just over the river, in the country. So I am a Yankee of the Yankees—and practical; yes, and nearly barren of sentiment, I suppose—or poetry, in other words. My father was a blacksmith, my uncle was a horse doctor, and I was both, along at first. Then I went over to the great arms factory and learned my real trade; learned all there was to it; learned to make everything: guns, revolvers, cannon, boilers, engines, all sorts of labor-saving machinery. Why, I could make anything a body' wanted—anything in the world, it didn't make any difference what; and if there wasn't any quick new-fangled way to make a thing, I could invent one and do it as easy as rolling off a log. I became head superintendent; had a couple of thousand men under me. . . . With a couple of thousand rough men under one, one has plenty of that sort of amusement. I had, anyway. Hank Morgan, the "Connecticut Yankee.[8]

Mid 1920s:

> The foreman is commonly the sole administrative agency of the shop. He is expected to look after tools and machines, find material and supplies for his men, instruct them in the manner of doing work, arrange tasks so that everyone is kept busy, enforce a proper pace, write up job cards and other records, preserve order, make orders and reports as requested concerning the progress of individual jobs, and give an opinion on which to base promotions and discharges.[9]

Mid 1960s:

> In summary, the foremen in continuous and job-order manufacturing have managed to maintain their status position while foremen in intermittent manufacturing have suffered a declining status. In large part, the relatively higher status of the foremen in continuous and job-order manufacturing is attributed to the fact that the skill level of the people they supervise is high. Other factors are at work here, of course, but the level of skill of these supervised appears to be the crucial determinant of the foreman's status in industry. Hence, the higher the skill level supervised the higher will be the foreman's status.
>
> In the sphere of intermittent manufacturing, the determinants which have lowered the foreman's status can be singled out easily. Manufacturers in this category have been diligently engaged in rationalization, which in part involves the specialization of labor.
>
> For production jobs specialization means constant simplification, leading to a decrease in the skill levels required of operating employees. *Lowering operative skill levels naturally affects the amount of skill needed by the foreman.* At present the foreman in intermittent manufacturing supervises only a fragment of the total production process and heads a department employing semiskilled or unskilled workers.[10]

These three excerpts are not offered as universally accepted definitions of the role and status of the foreman during various periods but as a rough indication of how that role

---

8. Mark Twain, *A Connecticut Yankee in King Arthur's Court* (Harper & Row, 1889), 5.
9. Edward D. Jones, *The Administration of Industrial Enterprises* (Longmans, Green & Co., 1926), 268.
10. William G. Scott, *Organization Theory* (Richard D. Irwin, Inc., 1967), 345–47.

has changed. In fact, there could be sharp disagreement with Scott's position that a lowering of operator skill levels naturally tends to reduce the amount of skill required by the foreman. It can be argued that, as skill levels are lessened, workers from the lower end of the socio-economic scale are attracted to such jobs. This, then, increases the demands upon the human relations skills of the foreman.

THE FOREMAN'S ROLE TODAY

To understand the need for additional skills on the part of foremen, we need only look at the concern being evidenced today in industry in the areas of human relations, motivation, sensitivity training, etc. In the eyes of the workers who report to him, the foreman is definitely a representative of management. Similarly, upper management looks upon the foreman as being a member of the management group. The properly trained and motivated foreman has a sincere desire to be honest and fair with his workers. Not only does he respect their trust and confidence in him, but he also does his best in representing their interest to management. On the other hand, he has been selected by management to implement management's planning and direction by organizing his work group and by establishing a work plan to achieve management's objectives.

In some respects, it can be said that the foreman is more than a manager and supervisor. Not only is he responsible for carrying out the orders of management, but he is also responsible for assuring that the employees fully understand the policies and goals of the company. This is of particular importance. No matter how well intentioned these policies and goals are, they will be of little value unless properly interpreted by the foreman, and carried out willingly . . . without discrimination. Thus, we see how the foreman has become the direct communication channel through which policies flow from management to the worker. Regardless of how well conceived company policies may be as established by higher management, it is the foreman who has the most effect on the reaction of the workers to these policies and the mental attitude of the employees toward the company.[11] It is easy to see why the foreman is often referred to as the "shock absorber" between management and the employees.

Since the World War II era, considerably more attention has been given to the use of carefully considered management philosophies in the selection and training of foremen. This is not to say that management had not employed good practices in the training of foremen prior to World War II. Some companies began the use of scientific management principles as early as the turn of the century. However, it has been only recently that industry has begun to consider the foreman a full-fledged member of management rather than simply an "overseer" of the work force.

The complexities of modern manufacturing seem to be increasing rapidly. On one hand, many innovations, such as new and advanced machine tools, numerical control, automation, and the computer, have been developed to improve efficiency and control of operations. On the other hand, the human factor has become highly complicated (it would seem) as compared to the past. For example, in the past, the responsibility of the enterprise was to make an honest profit by producing a needed good or service. Complications such as ecology, social responsibility, and governmental controls certainly were not as pressing.

In recent years we have also seen broad sweeping changes in our mores and customs, changes that are quite disconcerting to those accustomed to more traditional ways of

---

11. H. B. Maynard, *Effective Foremanship* (McGraw-Hill, 1941), 8–10.

thinking. These developments, along with the increasing complexity of manufacturing technology, have made obsolete the principles of foremanship which were workable two or three generations ago. As a matter of fact, unless a foreman embraces the concept of education involving a lifetime of learning, he is very likely to become obsolete in a relatively short time. While the new manufacturing methods have simplified the foreman's task in many respects, the proper use of these new techniques require more of him than did the older methods. Also, in the never-ending race for improvement in operational efficiency, his duties are apt to be constantly expanding.

Today, a fairly clear concept of the foreman's role in management is beginning to emerge. To explain the role, consider the following:

1) The highly technical activities under the supervision of the foreman have been assigned to staff specialists. Engineers design the product, and other engineers develop the processes and tools. Trained specialists in other disciplines secure the materials and provide the personnel necessary to manufacture the product. Industrial engineers plan and schedule the work. In short, technologists and specialists are employed to provide much of the instructions and resources which are needed at the point of manufacture to create a product or a service.

2) It is becoming increasingly clear that the residual responsibility for uniting all of these resources at the point of creating goods or services belongs to the foreman. He has become less and less involved in, and responsible for, planning, procuring, and coordinating and more involved in "putting the pieces together."[12]

A LOOK TO THE FUTURE

With respect to the future goals of the foreman, it is obvious that the Industrial Revolution continues. We need only look about us and observe the scientific and technological discovery of the past two or three decades to realize that we are experiencing a revolution. And it is a revolution in the same sense as when the term Industrial Revolution was used to describe the great upheaval which resulted during the eighteenth and nineteenth centuries from the technical advances of that time. Just as the earlier revolution completely altered man's way of living through significant social, political, and economic changes, today's revolution continues to create these changes.

The Industrial Revolution that started two centuries ago was called a revolution because it resulted in a new way of life for mankind. Its impact upon history was much more than the impact of the steam engine, the railway, the power loom, and the cotton gin. Although the effects of the revolution were great in the areas of mass production, the creation of new wealth, and the reshaping of world politics, still its most significant effect was the enormous social change which resulted.

The scientific revolution of the twentieth century gives promise of effecting greater technological and social change than the Industrial Revolution of the eighteenth century. The rapidly emerging new technology of today and tomorrow will have a far greater effect upon society than did the machines and processes of yesterday. In the coming decades an endless series of scientific and technological changes, especially advances in the computer and information communications technology, will be occurring.[13]

---

12. Joseph R. Ryan, "Foreman Activity Studies," from a paper given to ASTME Seminar, November 29, 1966.

13. John Diebold, *Man and the Computer* (Praeger Press, 1969), 4.

As we have said, the highly technical portions of the foreman's job are increasingly being assigned to staff specialists. This practice will probably be accelerated in the future, with the foreman continuing to be\responsible for the coordination of the material and human resources required for the performance of his work. It is the latter, the human element, which will be most affected, or perhaps *disrupted,* by the rapid and profound changes of the new technology. Just as computer technology affects the compilation, storage, and communication of information, it also affects the people working for the foreman. Information is at the very heart of our society, and its use significantly affects everyone. Today we are using communications technology in only a very elementary manner. It can safely be said that few yet understand the full capabilities and impact of this new technology. One thing, however, is certain; the role of the foreman-manager will change as the role of new technology is intensified. Just as the Industrial Revolution took man from the fields and brought him into the plants, so the new technology is moving workers from the plant into the laboratory and office. Today's foreman, and the would-be new foreman, must be aware of and adapt to this fast-changing technological environment.

PROBLEMS OF FIRST-LINE MANAGEMENT

Any discussion of the role of the foreman in industry would be incomplete without at least a cursory examination of the problems of first-line management. If we were to conduct a survey of a selected group of foremen and ask them to state their current problems, we would probably find that the list would contain most of the traditional problems. But it is likely that we would also find some new and serious problems. Certainly the "old favorites" of part chasing, missing or broken tools, machines that do not work, insufficient manpower, and so forth, would appear on each foreman's list. But if we were able to look beneath the surface, and if the foremen were able to take a long range view of their situation, they would probably say that there were two principal problems: (1) a lack of communication with management, and (2) a lack of management support.

In survey after survey, foremen have repeatedly mentioned that lack of communication is their principal problem. And when we examine the other types of problems experienced by foremen, i.e., part shortages, tool problems, manpower shortages, etc., it is easy to see that poor communication is frequently at the root of these other problems. Often, from the foreman's point of view, he has told someone about the problem, and nothing has happened. Frequently, the someone who was told either did not understand the problem, or did not respond properly.

Similarly, the foreman's problem of lack of management support, while often a real problem, is usually related to the problem of inadequate communication. Lack of management support is usually mentioned in connection with the disciplining of employees for infractions of company rules and regulations. In many instances, the foreman's view from his perspective on the production floor is limited; he is often unaware of many circumstances available to his manager or the cognizant staff representatives. Likewise, the staff personnel and middle-level production management do not always see the facts as they appear to the foreman. When higher management decides to revoke an earlier disciplinary action initiated by the foreman, the foreman's immediate reaction is to feel that he has not been supported.

Problems of first-line management as viewed by middle and upper management take on a different hue. The organization's failure to meet production goals, cost objectives, or established quality level is often blamed upon the foreman. Management usually feels that these goals have been properly established and clearly communicated to the foreman via whatever channels are normally used for these purposes. When the goals are not met, management may look to its first-line management as the cause of the problem. In cases like these, it is easy for management to assume that the first-line management team is inept, that it is taking sides with the workers, or that it is not sufficiently aggressive. While it is true that one or more of these reasons may sometimes be responsible for failures, it is equally possible that higher levels of management have not been given all of the information necessary to make a proper assessment of the case. Again, inadequate communication is the problem.

Workers do not perceive the problems of first-line management in the same light as the foreman and his manager. There is a tendency for individual workers to blame the foreman for all the problems with the company. This is only natural, as the employee sees the foreman as representing all of management. There is a general desire on the part of employees to have a greater say in decisions affecting their work. This, of course, makes the job of the foreman more difficult. Workers often chafe under supervision and resent "too much supervision."

The foreman today must have more intelligence, understanding, and people sensitivity than ever before. To satisfy management, he must keep his workers reasonably happy, and still achieve all the production, quality, and cost goals he and higher management have established. And all of this must be achieved within the terms of the union contract! In a later chapter of this book, the foreman's relationships with his workers as union members are discussed in detail.

The effectiveness of the foreman is in large measure dependent upon the cooperation and performance of others over whom he has relatively little control. For example, the effectiveness, or lack of effectiveness, of production control, manufacturing engineering, plant engineering, and quality control can make or break a foreman. These other areas critically affect his relationships with those he supervises and with those who supervise him.

No review of the many problems of first-line managers would be complete without acknowledgement of the current effort on the part of industry to provide employment for members of minority groups and other segments of the population formerly considered unemployable. Within this category are included ethnic groups such as Negroes, American Indians, Mexican-Americans, West Indians, inner city dwellers, hard-core unemployed, people under 21 years of age, the disabled, and high school dropouts. While the extra efforts being made today to employ these workers are necessary and extremely worthwhile, failure to recognize the attendant problems can lead to the failure of such programs.

From the foreman's point of view, there is an immediate need to understand the personal problems of these new employees. In many instances, companies have lowered their hiring requirements in order to allow the new employee to pass tests which formerly prevented him from being hired. The foreman must recognize the necessity of giving extra attention to such employees. All too often the employee has never before held a regular job; he may never have worked inside a building before, may never have had to get up at a regular hour, or may never have ridden public transportation to and from his home.

In addition to the problems concerning work habits, the foreman must also be prepared to handle the problems of antisocial behavior which years of economic and cultural deprivation may have created. Cultural problems, behavioral problems, etc., are all very real and it will be necessary for the foreman to be very sensitive to these areas.

Fortunately, government, business, and management are giving some priority to the problems associated with the employment and subsequent training of minority and disadvantaged workers. Numerous government and business agencies and alliances have been formed to assure the success of this gigantic national undertaking. One result of this effort is that various aids are being supplied to the foreman to help him make the programs successful. Some of the new approaches being tried include additional training periods, extra relief or utility workers, assignment of a "buddy" to the new worker to help indoctrinate him, and additional supervisory training for the foreman to increase his understanding.

All in all, management is probably doing more to assist the foreman in this undertaking than in any other area of first-line management responsibility. How successful these programs will be is a matter for speculation at this time. In some respects the success of attempts being made to integrate the minority worker into this country's workforce is directly linked to the success or failure of our political and economic system. Whether or not every approach tried in this area succeeds, the stakes are so high that we cannot refuse to make the effort.

It would be an oversimplification to state that all of these problems could be resolved by improved communications. However, many studies have revealed that improved communications can significantly improve relationships in other areas. The expression "breakdown of communications" is often heard when things go wrong, whether in a business, social, or personal situation. This phrase may be overworked, but too frequently it is the best explanation for failures.

Managers and supervisors frequently encounter trouble because of barriers to effective communications. Analytical studies indicate that the time of top business administrators is almost wholly absorbed in communicating—speaking, writing, listening, reading, and thinking. Middle and lower management personnel also devote the bulk of working hours to the process and problems of communication.

Effective communication enables a manager to train people, coordinate their functions, and lead individuals to work effectively to accomplish operating objectives. The manager who is a successful communicator improves employee morale and performance and thereby contributes to efficient, profitable operations. Two observations on the importance of effective communicating to the success of the manager-supervisor are worth repeating:

> Great masses of men work constantly at points below their top capabilities. We must help them to rise to their opportunities. One way to help is through effective communications, to motivate men to help achieve the goals of the company.[14]

> Social scientists tell us that employee understanding and loyalty do not come solely from hearing facts. Appreciation and loyalty result from self-expression in a situation in which the subordinate feels there is personal sympathy toward him and his views. Therefore, the superior should encourage subordinates at any level to ask questions and contribute their own ideas. Above all, he should listen, sincerely and sympathetically with intention to use workable ideas that are proposed.[15]

---

14. Henry Ford II
15. Earl G. Planty and William Machaver

The job of manager is to get things done through people. Effective communication is an essential tool for a manager in getting things done through people.

SUMMARY

The foreman today is definitely a part of management. As a member of the management team, the foreman is expected to:

1) Deal with personnel problems
2) Get the work out on time
3) Maintain quality standards
4) Keep his costs down
5) Improve methods

Similarly, the employees reporting to the foreman expect certain things from him:

1) Fair and equitable treatment
2) Wages consistent with others doing similar work in the community
3) Good working conditions
4) An understanding of their problems
5) To be treated sympathetically[16]

It can easily be concluded that there is no real conflict among the expectations and objectives of the foreman, his management, and his employees. That which is good for the employees is also good for the company, and that which is good for the company is also good for the employees. Anything that is harmful to one must be harmful to the other. The foreman, by the very nature of his job, is responsible for bringing management and the employees closer together.

In a survey done in a particular company to determine what people want out of their jobs, most of the foremen expected their workers to rate high wages as being important. Surprisingly enough, however, most of the workers did not rate wages as being particularly important. From a long list of possible choices most of the workers rated the following three items, in the order shown, as being most significant:

1) Getting along well with the people I work with
2) Getting along well with my supervisor
3) Having the opportunity to produce high quality work.

Assuming that his employees are like this typical group of workers, the typical foreman might conclude that getting along with others and doing good work are also important to his people. This survey is worth remembering. These two points, getting along with others and doing good work, fit in with a person's need to be part of a group in which he is accepted and which he himself accepts, his need to use all his capabilities, and his need to be recognized for the work that he does.[17]

While it may be argued that the status of the foreman depends on the skill level of those he supervises, it does not mean the demands on the abilities of the foreman

---

16. Carl Heyel, "Management for Modern Supervisors," (AMA, 1962), 10.
17. "The Successful Supervisor," New Century Program (Merideth Corp., 1969), 45.

are a function of the skill level of the workers. As the skill levels of workers are de-creasing, it would appear that the demands on the foreman are increasing. Due to the ever-increasing pressures to produce more goods at less cost, it seems the foreman is under pressure to produce more with less resources from which to draw. To you, as foreman, this "squeeze" means that the foreman's leadership talents are always being challenged.

The role of the foreman is undergoing constant change, both from a technological and a social point of view. Without seeming to assign a secondary level to the impor-tance of changes in the technology, the social changes experienced in the 1960s and 1970s will likely have a greater impact upon the foreman's job. A close examination of the responsibilities of the foreman will reveal that these social changes do not change his overall responsibilities. These social changes do, however, emphasize his "people" responsibilities.

The importance of the foreman's ability to communicate, listen, and be attentive to his "people" needs is clearly recognized by one company in its supervisory guide:

1) The successful supervisor deals with people as a group when the situation involves the whole group.
2) The successful supervisor leads the group through a democratic process to arrive at the best solution to the problem, although it may be easier to use force or pressure to get what he wants done.
3) The successful supervisor needs poise, self-confidence, and tact. He tries to prevent shyness and draws people into the spirit of the group.
4) The successful supervisor needs to keep aware of the changing roles within the group in order to use each group member to his best capacity.
5) The successful supervisor talks in terms of we, not I and you.
6) The successful supervisor gives orders with assurance.
7) The successful supervisor puts people at ease, by not being a threat or a fearful figure to his workers, in order to allow them to perform their best work.
8) The successful supervisor stands behind his employees.
9) The successful supervisor needs to be a good listener.[18]

The successful supervisor recognizes that it is important to develop team spirit among his employees. At the same time he must recognize that each member of the team is also an individual. He must also recognize that an employee's past experience and environment will determine in large measure how strongly he identifies with the group and joins in its activities.

We have identified the foreman as being a first-line supervisor and a member of the management team. In performing his job responsibilities, he is sometimes a foreman-supervisor, sometimes a foreman-manager, and—at all times—the company's first-line management representative. To the people who work for him, he is the company. In the same manner that the foreman wants to feel that he is a member of the supervisory group, so does the employee want to feel he is part of his work group.

One of the most important—if not the most important—means available to the foreman to assure success of his operation is a clearly identified open channel of communication. While technology and social changes may affect the role of the fore-

18. *Ibid.*, 73–74.

man, and while top managerial attitudes toward the foreman may have been character-
ized by indifference in the past, good communications will do much to alleviate these
problems in the future.

Finally, there is one very fundamental point for every foreman—whether new to
the job, or an older experienced man—to keep always foremost in his mind: *The
primary responsibility of the first-line foreman is the successful supervision of
people. It is in the discharge of this responsibility that he either stands or falls in
his job.*

Chapter 2

Transition to Management

Every few days in the typical large firm there is an announcement that a new person has been named to the position of foreman. This person may have been promoted from within the organization, he may be a young college graduate accepting his first assignment, or he may be a person with supervisory experience who has been brought in from another company. Whatever his background, the person placed in the position of foreman must go through a transitional period as he assumes his new duties and becomes part of the organization's management team.

During this transitional period the foreman must adjust to certain factors. These factors must be understood by the new foreman, his peers, and management in order to achieve an efficient and smooth transition. Accordingly this chapter is divided into three main sections: (1) personal adjustment, (2) compensation and status, and (3) personal development to meet new responsibilities.

PERSONAL ADJUSTMENT

One of the most important aspects of the transition to management is the personal adjustment which the new foreman must make to the new work situation. We will review three basic adjustments that the foreman has to make and discuss the problems involved with each. These three basic adjustments are work habits, relationships with other employees, and relationships with higher management.

Work Habits and Personal Characteristics

The newly promoted foreman should demonstrate such qualities as punctuality, courtesy, neatness, accuracy, dependability, patience, perseverance, health, energy, initiative, and aggressiveness.

His leadership capacity should be reflected in the high standards of performance that he establishes and maintains for his department. As pointed out in a later chapter, it is wise to develop standards, goals, and objectives in cooperation with operating employees. The foreman will be most effective if his personal characteristics inspire trust and confidence. The foreman should exhibit firmness. If he takes stands judiciously, he can stand firm on his final decisions and obtain cooperation. He also needs the quality of fairness.

17

If he is both impartial and just he can win the loyalty of his employees as well as his peers and superiors. Integrity is also an essential. Employees and others will cooperate with a foreman whom they can trust.

The foreman needs to be a good decision maker. He should be decisive, that is, he should learn to make decisions quickly rather than lingering over them. He should make decisions that are consistent with past practice whenever possible, but he must not be afraid to change when there are benefits to be gained. The foreman should learn to rely upon his people for advice and assistance in decision making rather than ignoring the experience that they might be able to bring to bear on problems.

The foreman needs the qualities of consistency and tolerance. Consistency is necessary because employees want to feel that his past behavior will give an indication of what to expect in the future. Employees often feel that they cannot rely upon a foreman who is erratic and unpredictable. Tolerance is required because the foreman may have to deal with employees and others who hold ideas and beliefs different than his own. Failure to accept employees because of their personal differences can interfere with job efficiency and cause friction within the department.

To summarize, the foreman's work habits and personal characteristics should be such as to inspire trust and respect in his employees and associates. He must recognize that he is a member of the management team, and that he will be held to higher standards than he may set for his own employees.

Relationships with Employees

Another aspect of the foreman's personal adjustment is the problem of maintaining the proper relationship with his peers and subordinates.[1] The new foreman has the positional authority granted to him by a superior. Management has announced his new title, moved him to the proper office, and will back up his orders. With his new authority he can now sign certain papers, evaluate his subordinates, and approve or deny requests. Except in extreme cases, most of his peers and subordinates will recognize and accept his formal authority. But a man cannot build outstanding success as a supervisor on the basis of formal authority alone. Loyalty and respect are the chief means by which a supervisor achieves success.

To earn respect of his subordinates, the foreman should bear in mind several important points. He should not assume the role of "one of the boys" as he will not be able to maintain the respect that he needs as a member of management.[2] Being "one of the boys" has a tendency to involve the foreman in emotional and personal issues where he will not be able to make sound, rational judgments. The foreman who has been promoted from the line can no longer be part of the same clique that he was before being promoted. The younger college graduate likewise should not permit himself to become enmeshed in the interrelationships of his employees.

In establishing a good relationship with fellow employees the new foreman has a fund of sound experience to draw upon, such as:

1) Previous responsibility for getting others to work with him at home, school, church, clubs, lodges, sports, and previous jobs.
2) Appraisals of former supervisors and leaders, and seeing what was effective or ineffective, in working with people.

1. Eugene Marble, "Making the Transition," *AMA Encyclopedia of Supervisory Training,* 385.
2. L. R. Bittel, *What Every Supervisor Should Know* (2nd ed. McGraw-Hill, 1968), 17.

3) Experiences in observing other supervisors in giving directions, and noting how others responded to orders, requests, tone of voice, and clear or vague instructions.[3]

The new foreman is well advised in developing a working arrangement with his peers for the mutual exchange of advice, information, and assistance.[4] He should also establish relationships with the personnel of staff departments responsible for furnishing services to his department. He should likewise establish a sound relationship with his own workers. In this regard the new foreman may start with these basic points:

1) Keep discussions with employees impersonal.
2) Be approachable, but businesslike.
3) Keep a cool head in emergencies or when issues start heating up.
4) Admit when you don't know and try to find the answer promptly.

The new foreman must practice good human relations and yet at the same time remain aloof from his subordinates. When personal problems are affecting job performance the troubled worker should be referred to the Employee Relations Department.

Relationship with Higher Management

The foreman is expected to identify with management, and to accept the values of his superiors. Being informed, having current and authoritative information to use and impart is necessary for managers at any level to be effective. The foreman's position at the bottom of the chain of command makes him dependent upon fewer sources, so he must take action to make sure he is informed.

The foreman occupies a critical, pivotal point, and it is important that he carry out management's decisions in the most efficient manner. Many potential supervisors are not able to make a proper personal adjustment and find that they have accepted a position which is psychologically very difficult. The very survival of a new foreman often depends on his ability to accept the challenge and to achieve a balance between efficiency and personal well-being.

COMPENSATION AND STATUS

Of vital concern to any new foreman making the transition to management is the compensation received and the status attached to the new position. In order to attract the desired type of individual, the compensation must be equitable, along with potential for growth and advancement.

There has been a good deal written about methods and techniques for establishing correct, equitable pay rates for foremen. Influencing factors include: prevailing rates for the type of work, industry, and area; government edicts; worker productivity; economic position of the firm; labor supply; and unions. In larger organizations, jobs may be studied closely from the standpoint of duties, demands, knowledge, experience, education, training, physical effort, responsibility, working conditions, and the like. The salary method of payment is usually preferred over hourly wages for foremen. Part of this is brought about by the wage and hour laws which classify the foreman as an exempt

---

3. "Introduction to Supervision," *CPP 41-A,* (The Department of the Army; First Session), Item 5.
4. "Introduction to Supervision," *ibid.,* Items 2–4.

employee. Since most management people are also on salaried compensation, the foreman is placed in that category.

In setting pay rates for foremen many companies try to establish a differential of at least 10 percent over the highest paid hourly job in the department. There are many instances where companies have failed to keep the salary structure in line with changing conditions. This creates an inequity with the foreman receiving less than some of the workers reporting to him.

When management has a free hand to set wages and salaries, the pay scale may be announced or advertised with the job opening. The prospective candidate or employee then can accept the job at the announced figure. Some candidates or applicants, of course, may be in position to bargain for higher pay because of their qualifications or potential. A college graduate or highly experienced individual from outside the organization may be brought in above the normal starting base salary for the new foreman promoted from within the ranks of the company.

Determining the proper relationship between the new foreman's rate of pay and the rates paid to his subordinates is complicated by the impact of overtime.[5] It is frustrating to foremen for their subordinates to be receiving time and a half, and even double time, for overtime while their salary schedule calls for them to receive straight time or a fixed salary for the same number of hours worked. The salary structure and overtime schedule must be considered when structuring the foreman's salary, with a differential of approximately 10 percent starting rate, as mentioned previously. Finally, the foreman's compensation should be equitable in relation to salaries paid for comparable management positions within the company and with other companies in the local area.

Foremen may receive benefits not available to hourly-rated employees. In some of the more aggressive companies, and in some instances the smaller growth-oriented companies, foremen participate in compensation plans such as profit sharing, stock options, bonuses, and other incentive plans.

The fringe benefit package can be used to shore up the total salary differential. Emphasis is not stressed sometimes in pointing out the total impact of fringe benefits received by the new supervisor. A list of some of these fringes are: vacations, personal time for emergencies, extended sick leave, improved life and health insurance programs, improved retirement benefits, salary continuance during strikes or labor trouble, educational assistance plans, discounts on company products.

PERSONAL DEVELOPMENT TO MEET NEW RESPONSIBILITIES

The old-time foreman ran his department single-handed. He fired and hired, meted out discipline, and scheduled and inspected work. He had no unions to deal with, and had few company and government regulations to follow. And his company was less likely to be concerned with national and international competition.

The foreman of today must be one who can understand changing technology and interpret it to new employees. He must maintain the morale of the old workers who find it increasingly difficult to perceive their individual contributions to mass production or modern production methods. An informed and understanding supervisor is particularly needed in this present era of advancing technological changes and the "new breed" of worker.

Most new foremen will possess some of the necessary qualifications for meeting new

---

5. A. Q. Sartain and A. W. Baker, *The Supervisor and His Job*, (McGraw-Hill), 9.

responsibilities. And it cannot be said too often that the new foreman is largely responsible for his own self-development, no matter what the efforts are by his superior and company sponsored programs. The self-development plan should be prepared by the foreman himself to prepare for the present and the future. The plan should be given strong emphasis not only during the transition period, but at all times. Shown in Table II-1 is a form for foremen to use in rating their progress in self-development.

Two broad categories of company-sponsored personal development are in-plant activities and other company sources. A combination of both sources is best, but often depends on the subject matter, location of the plant, and time available within the industrial or educational organizations.

Table II-1. Rating Form for Evaluation of Self-Development Efforts.*

	In Your Work	In Your Personal and Family Life
In the past Year		
1. Did you take formal training or instruction to further your progress?	_____	_____
2. Did you step up your reading?	_____	_____
3. Did you increase your participation in group activities (company teams, civic associations, church groups)?	_____	_____
4. Did you improve your ability to handle routine and repetitive activities (correspondence, putting up storm-windows at home)?	_____	_____
5. Did you at any time review your past activities to determine which are desirable, which ought to be dropped?	_____	_____
6. Did you find it easier to deal with people?	_____	_____
7. Did you have fewer emotional flare-ups?	_____	_____
8. Did you get greater enjoyment out of periods of relaxation and recreation?	_____	_____
9. Did you devote more time to thinking about the reasons other people behaved the way they did?	_____	_____
10. Were you more likely to concentrate on one activity until it was complete?	_____	_____
11. Did you devote more time to, and get greater satisfaction out of, helping others solve their problems?	_____	_____
12. Did you improve any of your skills or develop new talents?	_____	_____
13. Did you come up with some new conclusions about yourself, your personality, your habits?	_____	_____
14. Did you go in for new and more varied activities, develop new friends?	_____	_____
15. Did you find yourself making a larger number of independent decisions?	_____	_____
16. Did you find it easier to live with problems for which you had no immediate solutions?	_____	_____
17. Did you change some of your opinions and feelings about things?	_____	_____
18. Did you show a willingness to expose yourself to new experiences?	_____	_____
19. Did you gain a clearer conviction and a better understanding of the basic truths, religion, or philosophy in which you believe?	_____	_____

*Research Institute of America, New York

Company sponsored in-plant personal development of the new foreman may be accomplished in a number of ways:

1) The supervisor who has been promoted, and who directs the work of the new foreman, may be responsible.
2) If the former supervisor is not available—i.e., because of transfer, resignation, retirement, etc.—the department head may be responsible.
3) Some companies use performance appraisals, or require that goals be set, for accomplishing personal development or determining training needs of the foreman.
4) Company sponsored on-going orientation meetings may be conducted by company personnel, with question/answer periods, on similar topics as:

Budgetary control	Manufacturing production
Company organization	Manufacturing engineering
Cost accounting	Marketing-sales
Economics	Methods, procedures
Employee relations	Plant engineering
Engineering	Production planning
Industrial relations	Purchasing
Inventory	Quality control
Maintenance	Safety and health

In-plant training and development programs for the new foreman may cover such topics or areas as:

Human relations	Problem solving
Leadership	Decision making
Conducting meetings	Communications
Methods improvement	Motivation
Report writing	Evaluating workers
Job instructions	Accident prevention

The above-mentioned company-sponsored programs are generally tailored to specific problem areas associated with the plant or industry in which the supervisor is employed. Since these programs usually deal with specific problem areas, the new foreman is usually motivated because he can see the direct benefits to be gained from such programs. Supervisors often resist theoretical courses unless they are themselves pursuing formal courses in a self-developmental program, or unless they are college graduates.

Table II-2 indicates the kinds of programs a typical group of foremen felt were important to assist them in their jobs. Table II-3 shows the results of a survey in which foremen were asked to state the subject areas in which they felt they needed knowledge in order to perform their jobs. The data supplied by these two research surveys should be considered by companies in the process of establishing programs to assist in the training and development of first-line supervisors.

There is a wide range of self-help aids available to the new foreman. For example, the supervisor can take advantage of correspondence courses; programmed-instruction courses; join foremen, professional or technical societies, and participate in various activities of these organizations; and subscribe to magazines, journals and newsletters giving

Table II-2. Kinds of Programs Foreman Feel Are Needed.*

	Totals (n = 3868)	
Program	Number	Percent
Company Training Programs	3117	80.6
College Credit Courses	2800	72.4
Non-Credit Courses	1033	26.7
Workshops or Seminars	2080	53.8
Correspondence Courses	752	19.5
Other	17	.4

*Foremen in Indiana Industries (Manpower Report 70-C, Purdue University, School of Technology, 1970).

up-to-date information of special interest. These aids can enrich one's background and improve basic supervisory skills.

Adult and continuing education courses are quite popular, and are available in high schools in the evenings and in vocational-technical community or junior colleges. These courses and programs are often designed to fit in with the needs of the local industries. The advanced form of personal development for the new foreman would be in formal education which is also becoming more prevalent with industrial firms. Colleges and universities are also designing curriculum and degree plans especially to satisfy the needs of business and industry. These institutions are usually within easy reach of those desiring to advance their educational standing. Seminars, clinics, and workshops are also conducted by many and are promoted by advanced institutions.

The overall background of each supervisor should be taken into consideration before designing any specific personal development program. Such factors as prior supervisory experience, educational level, type of industry, and sophistication of product are a number of variables that need to be considered when designing a personal development program for any specific individual.

The majority of large, and many small, companies are now participating in educational assistance programs which pay all or part of the cost of tuition and books for employees working to improve their education. Such plans give the supervisors an incentive for participating in correspondence, programmed-instruction, adult or continuing education, college/university, or other educational programs. This assistance alleviates some of the hardship that might be experienced financially, and the programs also pro-

Table II-3. The Type of Knowledge Foremen Feel Is Desirable in Performing Their Jobs.*

	Totals (n = 4,221)	
Subject Area	Number	Percent
Human Relations	4,104	97.2
Communications	3,413	80.9
Personnel Functions	3,113	73.8
Production Planning	2,899	68.7
Methods Improvement	2,882	68.3
Quality Control & Inspection	1,937	45.9
Material Handling	1,530	36.3
Other (Miscellaneous)	124	2.3

*Foremen in Indiana Industries (Manpower Report 70-C, Purdue University, School of Technology, 1970).

vide a way of recognizing formally that the individual is making an effort to improve himself.

Supervisors often fail to realize the opportunities available for personal development through participation in various community activities. Church activities, school programs, voluntary organizations, service organizations, and political campaigns are particularly worth mentioning. The supervisor might assume certain managerial type responsibilities in these organizations. This can provide him with additional insight and understanding in solving some of the same types of problems which occur in his own organization. The supervisor is also able to acquire and develop confidence and skill in public speaking, human relations, organizational planning, and leadership. Because the public does not differentiate between front office and shop management, public and community relations are a supervisor's responsibility. As a representative of management, what he says and how he says it will be judged.

Some companies fail to encourage their line supervisors to participate in such community affairs as the United Fund Drive. The normal tendency is to assign other management personnel who can "be released from the job more easily," to participate. A greater sense of unity, as well as increased personal development for line supervision, would result if organizations promoted line-supervision participation in these and similar affairs more vigorously.

SUMMARY

The new foreman in his transition to management is expected by his superiors to achieve higher production, and is pressured by the workers to relax demands. He is cautioned by the personnel department to be conscious of human relations, and reminded by his superiors again of the need for discipline. Neither the organization nor the personnel working within the organization benefit if the new foreman finds himself caught in such a situation. Both will benefit if he is able to reconcile these conflicting forces as he makes the transition.

Strong emphasis must be placed in the areas of personal adjustment, equitable compensation, recognition, and personal development for the foreman in the transition process. This must be done effectively and successfully in order for the new foreman to fulfill organizational goals and assume higher management responsibilities. It is an accepted fact that "a chain is only as strong as its weakest link." The importance of the new foreman making a smooth and effective transition to management cannot be overstressed.

Chapter 3

Organization and
the Foreman

The foreman does not work alone; he is a part of a group, including the workers in his charge and a hierarchy of managers to whom he reports, who comprise the organization. The foreman's effectiveness is greatly dependent upon his ability to work smoothly as a member of the organization. He needs to know how other organization members can assist him in the performance of his duties. He should be able to coordinate the activities and objectives of his work group with other groups in the organization for the attainment of common goals.

In approaching the concept of organization as it relates to the first-line supervisor, we will begin by discussing organization in a general sense. The assumption here is that we are dealing with profit-making organizations, and certain modifications would need to be made to make the following remarks applicable to other types of organizations.

An industrial organization has its beginnings in the pooling of resources for profit. To earn profits, a product or service has to be produced and marketed. This activity requires that the functions of the enterprise have an ordered flow, which in turn requires organization, even if only to create a precedence in the scheduling of events. As a business enterprise grows and acquires additional employees, functions become more specialized. Organization is needed to ensure that each specialized function is performed correctly and at the proper time and place.

Although the foreman is at the bottom of the administrative ladder (i.e. by location, not in importance) the way in which the hierarchy above him relates to itself has a substantial effect on his operations.

ORGANIZATIONAL THEORY

There are essentially two schools of organizational theory; the traditionalists and the modernists. The traditionalist point of view is well-known—you start at the top and fan out to the bottom. The chief operating officer has his staff, each member of which has his staff in turn, and on down the line until we reach the foreman. At each level the traditionalist speaks of the "span of control," how many people can a given head manage properly? This question applies at every level, from the chief officer to the foreman. It is of equal importance at every level.

25

In the traditional organization model every level is designated as a "communication link" between the echelons above and the staff below. This is illustrated in Fig. 3-1. This interpretation is particularly important in stressing that the whole organization merely serves to communicate the stockholder's objectives to the "chip-cutters" (the people on the production floor performing profit-making services or making salable products) and to relay the wants and needs of operating employees back up through the organization to the stockholders.

The traditional model also provides for an automatic interrelation of groups at each level, creating units in which conflicts can be resolved—at least in theory. Every level is a member of a staff group in which other responsibilities are represented. This mixture usually represents groups that have conflicts in operation. This could mean production and maintenance, maintenance and manufacturing engineering, or engineering and

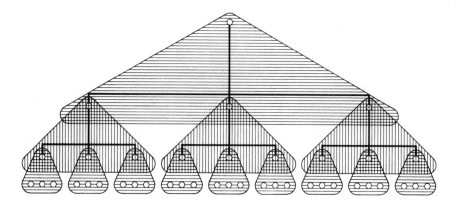

Fig. 3-1   Likert's depiction of the overlapping group form of organization. From Rensis Likert, *New Patterns of Management,* (New York: McGraw-Hill, 1961). p. 105. Used by permission of the publisher.

quality control. Bringing these groups together as members of a staff group permits an airing and, one hopes, a resolution of their conflicts.

We must hasten to insert here that a dyed-in-the-wool traditionalist represents another facet of an organization that is more psychological than mechanical. It's the "do-it-my-way-because-I'm-the-boss" syndrome; another symptom of which is "do-it-this-way-or-you're-fired"; or the "we're going to have a contest to see who can do the job my way best; the winner will get to keep his job" approach. The latter symptom is revealed in a pseudo-intellectual approach to resurrect a declining productivity. The sum of these techniques is to motivate by coercion and fear. It is older than the pyramids, and in today's socio-technological society it is just about as obsolete. In the vernacular of today's organization theory this approach has been labeled Theory X.[1] There are situations and individuals who are best handled by the use of Theory X, just as the rod must be used occasionally by a devoted parent. However, the results gained in applying Theory X are short lived, and for long-range results another approach is necessary.

---

1. Douglas M. McGregor, *The Human Side of Enterprise* (New York: McGraw-Hill, 1960).

At this point the modern theorist departs from the traditionalist. Whether or not he disagrees regarding the mechanics of the organization, he introduces Theory Y. As contrasted with Theory X, Theory Y involves a participative, consultative approach in dealing with employees. It's the "we have a problem: what can we do about it men?" approach. One of the most difficult aspects of this technique for the traditionalist to accept is permitting the work force to set its own goals. This method doesn't mean that they operate in complete anarchy, but rather that the constraints are given to the group as part of the problem. The objectives are also given to them, that is, a certain job must be done. How they will do it, exactly, and in what period of time, is left to the group to decide. Where this has been tried the evidence is that the group set higher production goals than management would have imposed. This approach has been tried with obvious caution and misgivings by management that had unfavorable experiences with bargaining units. We must add a note of caution in the use of this approach: it will not work where the objectives of the bargaining unit, in the labor-management game, is to reduce productivity and increase wages. It may be best to say that management's responsibility is to create an atmosphere in which capable employees are eager to perform superlatively.

Theory Y need not be taken quite this far, however, to achieve good results. Employees can be approached for their suggestions on how the targets can be met. Supervisors can, and should, become involved in their employees' needs. Too often it is the foreman who makes all the distasteful, painful demands on his people, while it is the bargaining committee that fulfills all of the pleasurable requests. When this dichotomy exists it is a symptom of failure in the organization and its ability to respond to its own needs. Company goals and employee goals can be brought together by the application of Theory Y, and the usual results are more highly motivated employees, less waste, higher productivity, and lower absenteeism.

The preference for Theory X rather than Y represents only one difference between the traditionalists and the modernists. The other conflict lies in their attitude regarding the hierarchical organization described earlier. Ultra-modernists maintain that the hierarchical, multi-leveled organization is obsolete, too rigid to respond to today's needs. Their answer is no organization at all. They support this approach by citing the negative response people give to being forced into a slot in the hierarchy. The hierarchy demands a chain-of-command action, stifling communications. A genius at the bottom of the hierarchy, with the one solution to a knotty problem faced by the man at the top, conceivably would never get his idea to where it would count. Even with each level responding conscientiously there would be significant distortion on the way up. The answer, say the modernists, is to do away with the hierarchy. Everyone can then communicate with everyone else. When a problem or project comes to this group, toss it to them and allow it to bounce around. Eventually, but in keeping with a schedule, a leader will emerge, and under his direction an organization will materialize to resolve the problem. A new organization will, theoretically, coalesce with each new problem.

Another parallel approach is to have the entire working group loosely attached, with those of a particular talent assigned to particular projects as necessary. This method is somewhat akin to the project management concept being used by many organizations today. The purists, however, maintain that the entire industrial organization can operate this way, and that the result will be more effective performance. There is obviously a great body of detail that must be arranged before such an organization is implemented. In today's hierarchical-organization culture this nonhierarchical technique should be approached with caution.

Organization Charts

Even among the traditionalists there is controversy. The organization chart, with its characteristic pyramid shape, implies that authority, responsibility, and decision-making power starts at the top and works itself down to progressively lower organizational levels (See Fig. 3-2). We mentioned earlier that the foreman is at the bottom of the administration hierarchy, and we pointed out that this has nothing to do with the importance attached to his job. This last note was a way of pointing out that there are those who look at organization charts and see a rank order of job importance. This thinking, unfortunately, is prevalent in organization chart analysis. Many companies, some of which are otherwise progressive in their management practices, refuse to publish hierarchical charts on the premise that it breeds inferiority complexes in those employees at or near the bottom of the chart. They feel that the confusion resulting from not publishing the chart and distributing it is less detrimental than the unfavorable attitudes which might result. This is a point of significant controversy.

An objection often raised against hierarchical charts is that they tend to establish rigid behavior patterns, resulting in a "that isn't my job" attitude. This, say the chart critics, diminishes cooperation between organizational units. The difficulty with this reasoning is that a cooperative spirit is neither enhanced nor diminished by a tool such as an organization chart. The real cause of a lack of cooperation is the operating atmosphere created by managers. An organization chart is a tool to be used in communicating with responsible personnel. Like any good tool, its absence makes the work a little harder and unnecessarily time-consuming.

Because of the dispute between proponents of organization charts and those who do not want them distributed, a solution has been offered in the form of a circular chart (See Fig. 3-3). The chart can be turned in any direction since there is no bottom. There is, however, a center—and the chief operating officer is at that point. When you turn the chart, everyone at the periphery is at what is the equivalent of the bottom of the traditional chart. The circular chart probably does not, however, solve the problems that some see as resulting from the dissemination of charts; rather it is a palliative that most likely does little good but likewise does little harm.

Organization charts, their updating and wide distribution are a necessity in a well-run organization. Although they are a static document not showing informal power ties or communication networks, they do serve as a starting point for the first-echelon supervisor in mustering support functions for the services he needs to produce.

ORGANIZATION AS IT AFFECTS THE FOREMAN

The foreman is the stockholder's front-line representative. Upon him rests the task of getting a return on the company's investments resulting from the plans, calculations, and decisions of officers of the firm from the president down. He has the responsibility of marshalling the services of others to provide the environment in which his group can meet production goals. The organization should be structured to respond adequately to the foreman's request for service. Unless his emergency and routine service requirements are met, the organization as a whole will not meet its objectives.

What kind of organization best fits the needs of the first-line manager? Ideally, it is that organization which gets the job done best, i.e., the one that most expeditiously and simultaneously provides those checks and balances that provide for automatic cost, quality, and schedule control. Does this mean that we first gather the personnel together,

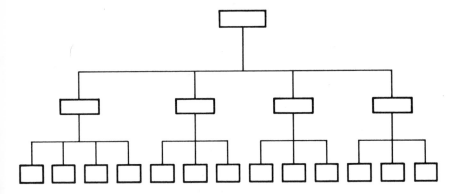

Fig. 3-2   Typical hierarchical organization chart.

Fig. 3-3   Circular organization chart.

review their related strengths and create the structure around them? Or do we, using good judgment and experience, create the required structure and then select people with the necessary strengths to staff it?

Establishing an organization around people requires three basic assumptions:

1) That techniques exist to evaluate personnel qualifications and determine staffing requirements
2) That, once established, organizational activities will somehow become routine and that appropriate procedures will develop
3) That the newly developed routines will be self-policing and self-auditing, resulting in satisfactory costs and schedules.

These may be poor assumptions. In the first place, there is no known technique for evaluating administrative strengths outside of a job responsibility situation. While many psychological and technical tests exist, some of which even profess to analyze emotions and other intangible factors, test results are at best only guides. Such tests cannot predict an employee's reactions under the multitude of pressures existing at any supervisory level in industry. A man may perform well on a given job; his next move, laterally or upward, may find him unequal to the task. Individual evaluations of a person's ability are tenuous at best; they are usually subjective and not based on accomplishment or contribution. Often an employee's ability is judged on the basis of his outward behavior—the faster he moves around the better worker he must be. The slow, deliberate, but more highly productive individual, who does his work with a minimum of difficulty, is frequently overlooked, or even considered lazy.

Anything beyond a one-man, or possibly a two-man organization, requires that routine communication be maintained if work is to flow smoothly. In organization of any size new procedures are slow in becoming routine and effective. Changing an organization to fit a personality would, logically, require that all procedures be changed to fit the new organization and the new personality. Does this mean that with every such change a new set of procedures is written? Certainly the system, whatever the organization, will develop some technique for handling work flow, but there would be much suspicion about its efficiency. To write procedures for this kind of change would be expensive, and perhaps a neverending task. The upshot of it all is that there would be no commonly recognized procedure; work would be accomplished only at the expense of efficiency and profit.

An organization based on personality invariably gives priority to the strong-man approach—"I'm here only because of the forcefulness with which I got my previous job done." It cultivates an empire-building enclave approach; it minimizes organizational cooperation and response. The result is that each organizational unit sets its own rules and establishes its own procedures; departments tend to go their own separate ways with no automatic checks and balances. Any system of checks and balances depends on a high degree of inter-unit cooperation. It exists only when an independent unit does the planning, another independent unit operates in accordance with the plan, and still another independent unit audits the activity. Such an organization does not result when restructuring is done to suit individual personalities.

There are two more noteworthy characteristics of structuring around people, both of which are detrimental. One involves employee attitudes, and the other personnel policy. In an organization which changes itself to accommodate personalities, employees are hard put to plan their career objectives within the company. The resulting confusion leaves them feeling apathetic toward the organization, or else they resign in search of greener pastures. The personnel department, in turn, has difficulty in planning for long-range staffing. Staffing requires a stable organization, a planned evaluation of accomplishment against organization objectives, and a planned rotation within and through the organization. Such personnel practices build strength in the organization and in people, but is impossible where personality is the pivotal characteristic in organizational structuring.

Now what of the alternative—creating a desirable organization and fitting people into it? The idea here is to conceive a workable organization based on organizational responsibilities, not on the personalities therein. If circumstances and times change, so must the organization; it must be dynamic to be successful. But once the concept is designed, personnel must be selected to fit it. Since most organizations are personality oriented, there may be little appreciation for fitting people to the organization—even though everyone talks about "fitting people to the job," and no one argues with that approach. The bridge to understanding how people are fitted to an organization is that a search is made for the strengths of people, not their weaknesses. Out of a given group of people, each has special interests and talents, usually well hidden among many minor interests and talents. It is this matching of special interests to an organization's needs that permits placing all employees into organizational roles in which they can contribute to organizational goals and objectives.

With organizational stability, employees know what is required by individual jobs. Training can be planned ahead, and the same training procedures can be used over and over again when new personnel are brought in. Systems and procedures become routine and thus are more easily learned and followed. Systems, operating costs, and improvements can be readily monitored and audited. Alfred Sloan, Jr., in his book, *My Years with General Motors,*[2] indicates that one reason for the success of General Motors was that the company developed a sound organization and staffed it with people who could do their jobs. There is little room to argue with that success. More currently, the management authority, Peter Drucker, advocates that people be fit into the organization[3], not the organization to the people.

SPECIFIC ORGANIZATIONS

Assuming that we have presented a convincing case for first establishing a good organization, and then staffing it, what would a good organization look like? We will assume, again, that the standard hierarchical organization chart has its advantages, and we will use it to present some concepts.

We will use a manufacturing plant for our model, without naming a product. What is illustrated here is valid with some modification for extenuating load conditions in the manufacture of discrete units. We will consider only that portion of the organization from the general manager down, since, generally, this is the area that affects the foreman's responsibility.

Fig. 3-1 illustrates what could be considered an acceptable organization for the greatest service to the foreman. It represents a minimum track for coordinating service activity. The only functions not falling under manufacturing is the procurement, scheduling, and movement of materials. These functions logically belong under one head, who is

---

2. Alfred Sloan, Jr., *My Years with General Motors.*
3. Peter Drucker, *The Effective Executive,* Bureau of National Affairs Film Series.

responsible for providing, to the production floor, the necessary materials, on time, in the scheduled quantities. The advantages to having these functions under a material manager outweigh the advantages of having them under the operations manager.

Variations from the format shown in Fig. 3-1 have been discussed at length in many volumes. Basically, the format shown provides the checks and balances we discussed. If staffed with anything less than professionals, the results will suffer. Variations from this pattern may reflect genuine disagreement with the concept. Such disagreements will occur; the point we have tried to make is that organization must be objective, not subjective.

SPAN OF CONTROL

"Span of control" is management jargon for the number of people or individuals one manager can effectively supervise. The exact number depends on many factors, some of which we will cover in the following pages. One important element, relevant to any one group being supervised, is the adequacy of communications. Assuming that the desired approach is the participative Theory Y concept, it is imperative that the supervisor take the time to establish rapport with his subordinates. Assuming there is no opposition to the principle that each employee be treated as an individual, the foreman must take the time necessary to learn enough to define each individual. He should evaluate the likes, dislikes, and needs of those he supervises. Clinical tests conducted by The University of Michigan Institute of Social Research[4] have shown that such an approach pays off in profits.

How many people, then, should a foreman supervise? By rule of thumb, the number is ten to fifteen. It could range from five to forty. Several factors will affect this ratio; for example it will certainly be affected by the skill level of the personnel being supervised. Skilled craftsmen generally require only work assignment and administration. On the other hand, craftsmen as a group occasionally decide to limit productivity for some reason. To overcome this practice it may be necessary to add supervision. Laborers especially on menial or tedious tasks, are on the other end of the supervisor's attention spectrum, requiring more frequent attention, thus limiting the number per foreman.

The degree and frequency of training a worker may require, and the frequency of decision making, affect the foreman's span of control. These factors must be tempered by the nature of the service or product being produced.

Motivation theory, as well as clinical verification, indicates that a foreman will get best results if he is people-oriented. This approach may require more of the foreman's time than task orientation, but the results justify that approach. He will spend much of his time inquiring about and resolving the problems of people. This is the application of McGregor's Theory Y.

The extent to which a foreman must audit the performance of individual workers will also affect the numbers he can properly supervise. This, in turn, depends upon the type of product being manufactured and upon the skill levels of individual employees. We must also account for the geographical area that must be covered by a foreman. There is a limit to how far a foreman can travel and still carry out his duties. Also, not to be overlooked as a significant variable is the foreman's personality. Whether formally or informally trained, his ability to motivate and manage people, above and below, will affect the number of people he can supervise.

---

4. Rensis Likert, *New Patterns of Management,* (New York: McGraw-Hill, 1961).

After considering these variables, we are confronted by the ultimate question. How much supervision will the budget allow? Increasing the number of employees per foreman from 10 to 20 will obviously reduce the supervision payroll by 50 percent, and reduce the effect of supervision proportionately.

The above factors are generally related to the types of people and product involved. What about the type of industry? Generally, the effect is as follows:

Fewer Employees Per Foreman	*More Employees Per Foreman*
Heavy industry	Light industry
Small plant	Large plant
Batch operation	Process operation
Low Volume	High volume
High precision	Low precision
Frequent changes	Rare changes

A heavy industry requires smaller crews using large equipment. A small plant creates its own limits because there are not enough people in a given classification to have many under one foreman. Batch operations have more frequent changes; problems of scheduling people, tools, and equipment, restrict the number of people to be supervised. A low-volume operation, even if continuous, may require that a single operator perform many operations, requiring greater attention from a foreman. High-precision operations require closer supervision than those of low precision. Operations having frequent product changes require closer monitoring of tools and more operator instruction.

UPPER AND LATERAL ASPECTS OF THE ORGANIZATION

At levels above the foreman the organization structure has greater depth and complexity. Complexity and depth are functions of the size of the organization. The foreman has little effect in shaping the structure above him. He is responsible to his immediate supervisor, who may be a general foreman or, in a small plant, perhaps the plant manager. Except for the service groups, upon whom the foreman calls directly for assistance, the general foreman is his link to the hierarchy. The organization of the service groups directly affect the foreman's ability to do his job.

These service groups include processing, industrial engineering, production and material control, transportation, maintenance, personnel, industrial relations, quality control, and accounting. They must be so organized internally that they respond effectively when their services are requested. These groups must provide routine services as well as emergency response. Tools, equipment, and raw materials must be provided according to schedule. Performance statistics must be made available in time to be used effectively.

For a service group to respond effectively, it must recognize and accept its responsibility, have good communication, and be adequately staffed. The relative weight of these factors is difficult to evaluate, but their complexity cannot be denied. It is pertinent to note here what the effect can be if service groups do not perform properly.

For example, when maintenance is performed poorly, the effects include increased downtime, frequent breakdowns, and increased costs. These are usually well-documented effects, permitting department managers to insist upon specific corrections. The one effect often overlooked in the face of poor maintenance is operator attitude.

Psychologists today are telling managers that they must satisfy employee needs. Each level of need must be satisfied before an employee begins to perform at a higher level. The objective is to develop performance at self-actualization level. It is here that the employee produced most effectively; good quality, efficiency, and satisfaction. But if the foreman does not communicate properly, or harasses the employee, his security may be threatened and his effective level of operation will drop. If a leak is not repaired and the employee must work with wet feet, or the drinking fountain does not work, the operator's efficiency drops to the level dictated by his physiological needs. It is the responsibility of every service group to contribute to maintaining the highest level of effectiveness.

Suppose the production control department fails to provide material to permit good use of production personnel? The effect is one of the most common, yet most weakening factors in manufacturing operations. In such cases, the foreman, either by mandate or frustration, usually begins operating as a stockchaser and expediter. He loses sight of his primary responsibility and wastes his time searching for stock and in other equally time-consuming activities. There are many instances in which the foreman even prefers this arrangement. It is easier to look for a skid load of parts than to act as a manager should and deal with employees and their problems. Whole factories are taken up by this mania. It is justified by the fact that "we must get the stuff out the back door." Completely over-looked is the fact that the system has broken down and some analysis must be made to produce a workable solution. The losses in profit resulting from such misassignment of responsibility is difficult to estimate.

The same kind of system failures occur in other service areas. Though often recognized by upper echelon management, there is often insufficient courage, leadership, training, and know-how to correct the situation. Summaries of productivity, expenses, and attendance must be provided regularly to the foreman. Training must be planned well in advance; bargaining effects must be communicated and explained routinely.

The foreman's immediate supervisor should create an atmosphere in which the foreman can freely express his needs and ambitions. With an open channel of communication, the superior can transmit company policy and objectives as well as receive the uninhibited comments of the foreman regarding operation policies.

Management above the foreman level must organize to see that the foreman's problems are, as far as possible, routinely recognized and resolved. Special calls for assistance should be expeditiously handled. Routine problem resolution requires standard systems and procedures, training in their use, and knowledge of their existence.

The foreman, upon being trained in the use of these standard systems and procedures, should exercise a personal discipline in their use. He must also exercise his responsibility to request changes in existing procedures as required for effective application. Systems and procedures are dynamic instruments of management. Where the foreman is affected and does not insist upon updating obsolete systems, routine and the expeditious resolution of problems will decay.

Upper management must also organize for line foreman involvement in decision making. It is commonly recognized that a supervisor cannot be held responsible for an occurrence, or lack of it, if he has no authority to control it. Management cannot ignore the line foreman when making decisions that will affect his area, layout, facilities, tools, or personnel. The foreman cannot conduct himself as a manager when he cannot exercise control over the forces affecting his job.

SUMMARY

On the traditional organizational chart for management, the foreman is on the bottom, but this in no way indicates his relative importance. The foreman is the link between management and the workers on the shop floor. He represents the workers to management, and he represents management to the workers. He is also the link between his department and the supporting groups, such as maintenance, upon which he must rely. In this position, the foreman is one of the most important links in the system, and he must have open communications with upper management, his workers, and the supporting groups.

Chapter 4

The Foreman's Job:
A Systems Perspective

In the preceding chapters we discussed the foreman in general terms. We evaluated various definitions, reviewed the historical background, and considered the foreman's role in the community. We examined the industrial environment in which the foreman functions in order to understand the stresses to which he is subjected.

In this chapter we will move in closer and focus on what the foreman does. We shall be looking at his responsibility in six specific areas:

1) Personnel supervision
2) Directing production operations
3) Quality control
4) Cost control
5) Equipment maintenance
6) Safety.

We will describe the nature and purpose of the major tasks which the foreman performs. We will indicate how these tasks contribute to the operation and improvement of interlocking management systems. Some consequences of successful and unsuccessful performance of the foreman will be presented to illustrate their importance in the total scheme. Lastly, we shall attempt to provide a foundation for succeeding chapters.

SYSTEMS AND THE FOREMAN

When we ignore, for the moment, all the theoretical descriptions of the foreman's job and actually observe how he spends his time and why he is involved in these activities, two factors stand out. First, the enterprise is usually organized to provide the foreman with all the resources he needs to produce. Second, the foreman spends most of his time in activities directly resulting from failure of the organization to actually deliver the needed resources. Study after study shows the foreman:

1) Chasing parts
2) Debugging production methods

3) Reworking parts
4) Writing up "hot lists" to correct computer printouts
5) Checking on the status of orders so Production Control can "plan" his schedule
6) Expediting the tools that tool engineering (or industrial engineering) told him he would have
7) Urging maintenance to repair a machine.

Today's line-and-staff organizational structures are based on the premise that the foreman combines the resources brought together in his department and produces goods or services within given cost, quality, delivery, and human relations requirements. When we examine the production segment of a modern manufacturing organization we do, in fact, find that it is a network of systems designed to provide the foreman with what he needs to produce a product or service.

Implicit in this definition is the responsibility of the foreman to anticipate and recognize breakdowns in the operation of these systems and to take appropriate remedial action. When the foreman does take such action, he is expected to notify those responsible for the system that he has done so.

This responsibility has its creative corollary; the foreman, on the basis of his experience and close association with the actual production of goods or services, is expected to contribute to the improvement of the system. This premise enables us to define more thoroughly the specific responsibilities of the foreman and relate them more directly to the objectives of the total enterprise.

The World of Systems

The foreman stands at a point where a number of systems converge. Each of these systems (with its subsystems) has been designed to deliver some resource to a specific area where it will be combined with other resources to produce a desired result. These systems can be classified in many ways. In this chapter we shall group them under the following headings: (1) the personnel system, (2) the production system, (3) the quality control system, (4) the cost control system, (5) the facilities system, and (6) the environment system. Obviously, this classification cuts across department lines and requires us to think of any system in inclusive terms. It is useful to take a closer look at each of these systems:

1) *The personnel system.* This system includes the recruiting, interviewing, and selecting of new employees, as well as the transferring of eligible employees; training or retraining, setting up and maintaining individual records; and negotiating and implementing labor contracts. Line management, the industrial relations department, and the personnel department are the principal management groups involved in the design, operation, and maintenance of this major system.

2) *The production system.* The production system provides the drawings, specifications, and processing instructions necessary to produce a part. This system also prescribes the schedules and provides the materials and supplies required to fabricate the product on time. Sales, engineering, purchasing, stores, production control, and line management all contribute to the production system.

3) *The quality control system.* The quality control system tests and inspects materials, components, processes, and finished goods to assure marketing a product which conforms to engineering specifications and meets customer expectations.

Sales, product engineering, process engineering, and quality control are all concerned in the function of this system.

4) *The cost control system.* This system requires inputs of data from receiving, stores, production records, timekeeping, payroll, and shipping. It digests, organizes, and publishes these data (with appropriate questions and comments) in the form of ratios, comparisons, and reports to inform management of trends, and problem areas.

5) *The facilities system.* The facilities system provides plant, machinery, and tooling as well as maintenance of these assets. It seeks to provide pleasant and healthy working conditions and to avoid pollution of the environment. Line management, process engineering, maintenance, plant engineering, production control, and industrial engineering, under the surveillance of the finance department, collaborate in the operation of the facilities system.

In this context, it can be seen that in all instances several departments are concerned with a system, its design as well as function. But it is even more apparent that the complexity of the systems (i.e., the number of departments and individuals involved) increases the potential for gaps between systems, system breakdowns, and organizational failures. This aspect of manufacturing life dictates, to a large extent, the foreman's job and explains why his action often departs from what management considers appropriate.

Each department is vitally concerned with its part of the system, and presumably each department is designed to interface perfectly with the other departments. However, this interface is almost always less than perfect, and systems analysts have long recognized that certain difficulties exist. They are diligently creating *total systems,* that is, systems which include every necessary step in a procedure. They seek to totally integrate all systems, regardless of primary or secondary objectives, with all other systems. Until this goal is achieved, we have to contend with four facts:

1) Systems and subsystems are not complete
2) Systems and subsystems are not self-monitoring or self-correcting
3) Systems do not always interface at key points
4) Systems will only operate successfully when individual workers fill in the gaps, correct errors, and provide interface.

Behavior in the Real World of Systems

Now let us turn our attention to the successful foreman's behavior in the real world of systems. These systems were designed to provide him with the resources he needs but sometimes seem only to present him with a never-ending array of problems. Observation of the foreman's role discloses three major activity areas consisting of operating, reporting, and improvement tasks.

1) *Operating tasks.* These consist of determining what needs to be done and doing it. This includes: (a) reviewing schedules, checking availability of prints, materials, tools, equipment, and personnel, and deciding what is to be done by whom, where, and when; (b) observing activities to assure that approved practices are being used, and that quality and cost standards will be maintained while meeting the time schedule; (c) anticipating systems failures which will cause material or manpower problems, taking corrective action, and communicating that action to those concerned.

2) *Reporting tasks.* Reporting tasks include two broad subdivisions, quantitative and qualitative reporting, with many specific tasks related to each. Quantitative reporting includes such tasks as reporting production, filling out scrap and rework tickets, shortage reports, and time reports, and writing transfer and reassignment slips. Qualitative reporting encompasses a wide range of more diverse acts, many of which will be verbal and concerned with cause-effect relationships. These tasks include recognizing difficulties and their consequences, ordering repairs and requesting adjustments to tools, evaluating schedules and estimating delivery dates, relaying labor difficulties to management, and submitting opinions on the performance of suppliers, tools, materials, and processes.

3) *Improvement tasks.* Improvement tasks include seeking ways to improve methods, materials, tooling, processes, and devising systems which will improve skills, performance, quality, and delivery, or will reduce waste, damage, cost, inventory, lost time, and effort.

It is the objective of this chapter to define, in practical terms, the specific responsibilities of the foreman. Before doing so, we have set forth a premise which provides the rationale for the discussion to follow. This premise is: *The foreman's function is to combine resources into goods or services within cost, quality, and delivery constraints; to anticipate and recognize failures in supply and support systems, to take remedial action, and to report such action. Nearly everything a foreman does is related to these systems, to the reporting of their results, and to assisting in their improvement.* We will now examine each system in more detail.

THE PERSONNEL SYSTEM

We saw earlier that the personnel system is designed to provide qualified workers who will function in a well-defined social organization. In most companies, this system cannot operate successfully without the foreman's contribution.

The personnel system is designed to:

1) Provide workers (from within the firm or outside of the firm) who are able or can be trained to perform the tasks required to manufacture the product.

2) Establish (unilaterally and/or through negotiation), publish, and implement equitable labor relations policies and procedures.

Manpower

Rare is the foreman who does not have to determine his manpower needs for himself. Using production schedules and labor standards, mentally adjusted by experience, he estimates his requirements not only in numbers of workers but also according to job classification mix. Industrial engineering, using labor standards and past performance data, can materially aid in preparing manpower requirements. He sets the dates when a change in the number of workers or a different mix of classifications are required. These predictions are reported in the form of requisitions and transfer or release notices.

The employee relations department acts on this information provided by the foreman. When additional personnel are required it posts notices of openings so that present employees can upgrade themselves; it screens candidates from inside as well as outside to assure that only reliable individuals with the necessary potential are considered.

Normally, the foreman then selects the individual to fill the job based on his own evaluation of the candidates. He tells the man he is hired or requests a new candidate. Once a candidate is selected, employee relations handles the necessary administrative work.

In cases where workers are to be transferred or laid off, industrial relations usually informs line management, including the foreman, who is to be transferred or laid off in accordance with company policy or the union contract. The foreman then must notify the worker and explain the reason.

In these areas of responsibility the system works quite well. It is the foreman who makes the most conspicuous mistakes in performance and judgement but not without reason, for he has many opportunities for error because of gaps in the system. For example:

1) He can neglect to consider the impact of an order on his manpower requirements.
2) He may miscalculate the number of workers necessary or the skills required.
3) He may be slow in informing the personnel department of his requirements, not giving them enough lead time to recruit workers.
4) He may not perform well in interviewing candidates and thus introduce incompetent or poorly motivated personnel into the work group.
5) He can permit a negative labor climate to develop which results in poor productivity, low quality, and high absenteeism and turnover.

Obviously, the first three opportunities can be prevented by eliminating gaps in the system. The fourth can be improved by providing training in interviewing employee candidates and by developing more meaningful criteria for determining a candidate's capabilities. Ways and means of avoiding the fifth will be discussed in later chapters. Suffice it to say here that without planning, skill, and considerable effort by the foreman, the employment phase of the personnal system will create mahy problems.

The reporting tasks related to the manpower aspect of the personnel system are usually confined to a few relatively simple forms such as requisitions, transfers and absentee reports. The foreman's principal contributions consist of helping to integrate the systems which determine the numbers and skills required to satisfy production requirements, and improving his own skill in interviewing and assessing candidates for jobs.

Labor Relations

The importance of the foreman in labor relations has been stressed in every conceivable manner since the passage of the Wagner Act in 1935. However, the foreman still may not be aware of what is expected of him. Let us re-examine the foreman's responsibilities in a broad sense from the standpoint of the tasks he must perform to make the company's labor relations program work.

The industrial relations department is usually responsble for developing and coordinating labor relations policy, whether or not these policies are set forth in the union contract. The foreman, however, is responsible for the success of labor relations policies which he often has little or no role in determining.

Managing his personnel under labor relations policy is probably one of the most frustrating tasks for the foreman. For example, he may have to keep written records of oral warnings to employees in order to justify a formal written warning at some later date; he may not be permitted to reward good employees with merit raises; and complicated overtime policy may require considerable planning and record keeping. The good foreman, however, accepts his responsibility and handles his tasks with proficiency. He knows the contract better than the union committeeman, he heads off grievances, and he gives his workers a fair deal. He is his workers' source of instant and reliable information on fringe benefits, insurance, promotional opportunities, earnings, and other matters important to their welfare, advancement, and peace of mind. The foreman's inability to answer these questions, which are important to his workers, often leads to a lack of respect for him by his workers.

It is not only the foreman's responsibility to implement labor relations policies and procedures, but also to observe their effect, evaluate their worth, and feed back his observations and recommendations to the industrial relations department. This is the only way that staff executives will learn of problems and consider changing policies to solve the problems.

PRODUCTION SYSTEM

The production system is designed to deliver a specified product or service to the customer at a scheduled time. With this objective in mind, the production system pulls together many interrelated subsystems. These subsystems range from the development of a bill of materials to materials management, process and production control, customer information, and finally shipping. To the foreman, production control appears to be the dominant part of the production system, but in reality the major part of the system operates beyond his horizon, including the roles played by engineering, and much of the work done by production control, purchasing, and process engineering.

Materials

The engineering department is responsible for preparing the bills of materials which are required for the manufacture of products. Production control, if it is responsible for materials management, will include purchasing, receiving and stores, scheduling, machine loading, expediting, internal materials movement, and customer relations. All of these sub-responsibilities, whether performed by production control or by other departments, are essential to the overall coordination of the delivery of materials to the work area.

The foreman is rarely involved in developing specifications and product requirements. He is, however, deeply involved when he begins to use the material to produce the product. At this time he becomes aware of the workability of the materials, and he becomes an excellent source of information which should be fed back to engineering, production control, and purchasing.

Staff Assistance

Methods, processing, and manufacturing engineering are responsible for determining the operations and their sequence for manufacturing the product. They design (and often manufacture) the tools and equipment needed. Industrial engineering, which may or may not be a part of manufacturing engineering, shares in the responsibility for determining operating methods and developing production standards and manpower requirements—all of which are important to the foreman. These departments combine their efforts to provide specified materials in the proper amount so that a quality product may be assembled and delivered on schedule.

Often, the effect of manufacturing engineering on the system is not appreciated. In the process and metal industries this role is extremely important and has been growing as profit pressures increase. The foreman's major responsibility is to see that process specifications are followed by his workers. Consequently, he finds himself continually monitoring his workers, giving them instructions or training when necessary, and correcting them when they fail to adhere to specifications. When he is not observing his workers, he is checking on the operation of tools and equipment in order to anticipate adjustments or repairs which will be needed.

In those companies which do not have manufacturing or process engineering departments, the foreman's participation in the fabrication of a product and the methods to be used by the worker is much more significant. Indeed, in many small speciality companies, the foreman is expected to be the expert in these matters, and his decisions and judgments are final.

Industrial engineering also participates in the production system; it provides operating methods, production standards, and manpower requirements, all essential to the operation of a viable production system. However, these operating methods will not be used, production standards will not be met, and manpower levels will not be adequate unless the foreman is actively engaged in teaching and motivating the workers and seeing to it that they have what they need.

Capable though they may be, industrial engineers rarely develop a "best method." Many times the foreman, in cooperation with industrial engineering, must work out a practical method. Changing methods and the movement of workers from job to job creates a never-ending need for operator training which must not be simply delegated to an experienced worker. It requires the attention of the foreman.

Just as industrial engineering does not always produce the best method, neither does it always produce equitable or acceptable production standards. When a worker objects to or fails to meet a standard, the foreman must assume the responsibility for checking it out. If, in his judgment, the standards are unrealistic, he should discuss it further with industrial engineering. If it is not resolved to the foreman's satisfaction the situation should be taken up with higher management.

Production Control

The production control department is one of the two or three groups with whom the foreman spends the most time and perhaps has the most difficulty. This situation results from conditions developed during the course of time.

The extent to which production is planned for the foreman can vary widely among companies, between departments, and even from one product line to the next. As planning and control have gradually become more pervasive, the degree of completeness with which scheduling is conducted has increased. In the past scheduling was done on a monthly or weekly basis. Frequently the early schedules simply showed what items were to be produced during a given time period. The foreman determined the priority of individual orders, and theoretically he sequenced orders to employ his people and equipment most efficiently. As machine and works station loading become increasingly necessary for optimum utilization of expensive equipment and facilities, planning and scheduling have become more exacting. Today, in many shops, the sequence for starting jobs, the operations to be performed, the machines to be used, and the time allocated for each operation are all specified in detail.

It is one thing to create a schedule and something else to meet it. The strongest pressure placed upon the foreman, next to keeping his department busy, is to "get the work out." Consequently, he devotes considerable attention to anticipating events which might disrupt his schedule or idle his employees. In many shops nothing takes precedence over these two responsibilities except safety. When a breakdown occurs the foreman must take immediate steps to repair equipment and frequently to invent some alternative method which will permit him to complete the operations in some other way or on some other piece of equipment. When materials do not arrive on time, the foreman himself must often decide upon the best alternative while the production control department works out a revised schedule.

Labor Performance

The fact that technical skill is needed to develop equitable labor and optimum process standards does not mean that the foreman is not important in this area. Since he is responsible for assigning men to jobs, teaching them to perform these jobs, motivating them to achieve standards, and disciplining them, he should be satisfied as to the fairness of the standard. Where the foreman is the recognized leader, standards engineers are technicians who appear, when requested, from the industrial engineering operation. A rule of thumb might be proposed: *The foreman's authority and prestige is inversely proportional to the worker's dependence on the standards engineer.*

Although the industrial engineering department has the responsibility for determining work methods and establishing work standards, it is clear that the methods will not be used nor the standards achieved without the foreman's participation in their development, implementation, and updating. Indeed, most industrial engineering departments depend on the foreman to tell them when new standards are required, when current standards should be changed, and when conditions exist which indicate the need to improve the method or reset the standard.

Generations of training directors have developed and conducted training programs designed to provide the foreman with the insights and skills necessary to maintain a high level of worker productivity. Many of these programs were constructed to satisfy needs which the foremen themselves defined. To this extent, foremen have participated in improving the design and structure of such programs.

QUALITY CONTROL SYSTEM

The objectives of the quality control system are, of course, to assure that the customer will receive the quality product promised him by the sales and engineering departments. Since quality is built into a product or service, it is necessary to begin the quality control system at the very beginning—during the product engineering phase.

In addition to designing the product, engineering sets the specifications for the materials, the tolerances for the parts, and the operating characteristics of the finished product. Manufacturing engineering establishes the process requirements and designs tools capable of producing materials and parts to specified standards. Quality control provides inspection for incoming materials, inspectors to check processes, and final inspection to assure that the product meets engineering specifications.

Product Engineering

On the surface it would appear that the foreman has little to do with delivering a well-designed product. On the contrary, however, he plays a most important part. In most companies the foreman is looked to for information which, when fed back to the engineering department, can assist in the alleviation of engineering problems. Many times this feedback consists of constructive criticism of specifications which have little or no effect upon quality. His experience in working with a wide variety of materials frequently enables him to suggest substitute materials or changes in specifications which can reduce costs while enhancing or maintaining quality.

Routinely, the foreman is responsible for using the materials specified in the design and ensuring that the workers are actually using the correct materials. Moreover, it is through his constant attention that the dimensional tolerances necessary to produce a final quality product are achieved. In many industries the foreman must have considerable knowledge and experience in order to detect when materials and/or work methods are responsible for poor quality.

Process Engineering

The foreman is usually more directly involved with process engineering's role in the quality system than with the product engineering aspect. Since process engineering furnishes specifications and provides the tools and equipment to meet these specifications, the foreman often spends time making sure that they are understood, observed, and adhered to by his workers. Moreover, he finds himself spending a great deal of time and effort in evaluating the performance of tooling and equipment, and attempting to discover why difficulties are being encountered.

Perhaps one of the most important contributions the foreman can make is to apply his expertise, acquired through years of practical experience, to searching out reasons and causes for rework and rejects, and communicating these to the proper engineering group.

Quality Control

The mere mention of quality control in the company of foremen often evokes a strong reaction. Despite the protestations of both sides, it sometimes appears that both the inspection department and the foremen enjoy the "contests" with which they become involved. These "contests" may be constructive, though in most cases they are not, and almost inevitably they result in negative behavior which does not enhance or assist in maintaining quality. Many programs and campaigns have been undertaken over the years to motivate supervisors and workers to improve quality. "Zero Defects" is an example of a recent program in this area. While these programs have sometimes failed, it should be recognized that attitude has much to do with producing quality products.

Hardly anyone, least of all the foreman, fails to recognize the dominant role the foreman plays in making the quality control system work. Through his efforts to develop skilled workers and motivate them to do their best, his struggle to constantly improve the performance of his equipment and tools, and his search for the causes of rework and rejection, the foreman makes it possible for the quality control system to function.

The importance of attitude provides the foreman with opportunities for improvement. Perhaps his first contribution in the achievement of quality can be made by acting positively in all matters related to quality. The aggressive and constructive foreman might fight many battles with engineering and inspection to prove that quality requirements or process specifications are not realistic, but he should never stoop to subterfuge or tricks to get his work passed.

The quality control system is frequently overlooked as a major source for cost reduction and product improvement. The product is usually designed to satisfy a narrow range of performance characteristics and when these characteristics are not met, the product is unacceptable to the customer or suffers in the market place. On the other hand, a product which exceeds established quality characteristics may do so at a cost which is too high for the segment of the market the company is striving to penetrate. It is frequently possible for the foreman to make methods improvement suggestions which may significantly reduce the cost of achieving a desired level of quality.

COST SYSTEM

The cost system is a means by which product costs are estimated, reported and controlled. Many foremen believe that the cost system is designed to harass supervisors who have no opportunity to defend themselves. Space is not available to analyze this belief in detail. We will have to be content with the statement that the system probably has other objectives which are more pragmatic.

The fundamental objective of the cost system is to provide control, in the sense of direction, not restriction. The system enables us to:

1) Make better decisions by comparing the estimated cost of various alternatives. These costs may have to do with products, processes, or quantities.
2) Set labor, materials, and expense cost targets for components, processes, and completed products.
3) Monitor costs as they accumulate and sound an alarm when deviations from targets reach critical levels.
4) Set targets for other expenses not directly related to manufacturing, such as engineering and sales expense.

As soon as it was discovered that literacy had replaced muscle as the major qualification for the foreman, paper work systems were redesigned. The foreman is often required to obtain and deliver accurate and understandable information to accounting, payroll, production records, and employment. Despite the more recent trend to have machines and people report for themselves by being wired into electronic communication systems, the foreman is still important in this area.

Many departments are involved in the total cost system. However, the foreman is most directly concerned with timekeeping, production records, and cost accounting (or budgeting). We will confine our discussion of this system to these segments of the cost system.

Timekeeping

Because the time spent by workers is charged to products or jobs, timekeeping is an important aspect of the cost system. To the extent that the input data are incorrect, resultant cost reports will be directly affected. Accumulations of errors in time reporting can degrade the cost reporting system to the point where it becomes meaningless to management.

It is the foreman's job to see that time is accurately reported by the worker and that the correct order numbers and job numbers are used so that reliable data will be fed into the system. In addition, the foreman can make an important contribution to the improved operation of the time system because through good communications with his workers he can develop acceptance of the need for these data being accurate.

Production Records

Perhaps this subject should be combined with timekeeping since in many companies it is used in a single expression—time and production reporting. Obviously, accurate production counts are needed to develop reliable cost data since this is the factor by which production time is divided to arrive at the time per unit—the basic element in manufacturing cost accounting. As a rule greater accuracy is achieved with production reporting than with time reporting, perhaps because in most companies it is easier to "count pieces" than it is to count minutes. Nevertheless, obtaining accurate production reports is one of the major headaches a foreman must deal with from one day to the next. It is important for him to be able to effectively discharge his responsibility by submitting accurate production records on time, to be fed into the daily production and time reports.

Cost Accounting

Perhaps the most important part that the foreman has to play in the cost system is the continuing battle to keep costs within budgeted limits. From the foreman's point of view it sometimes appears that the whole cost system has been designed to embarrass him. It is not surprising that he reacts in this way becuase he stands at the point where costs most frequently exceed budget. Also at this point there is often little that can be done to recapture losses since as the parts are made production time has been spent on them.

Although it may not be readily apparent, the foreman can make a significant contribution to effective functioning of the cost system. In the first place, he plays an important role in establishing the performance standards used in developing cost estimates. He can help industrial engineering not only in developing these data, but also later in achieving cost objectives through his ability to get his workers to produce at standard.

From cost data it becomes possible to establish labor, material, and expense budgets which are used to plan and later monitor the performance of the manufacturing department. These data are usually assembled by the department, or in larger companies by a budget department, from forecasts made by the several operating departments. In many companies the foreman participates in developing the portion of the budget for which he will be held responsible.

In fairness to other departments, we should say that many of them are beginning to feel the same kinds of cost control pressures the foreman has experienced over the years. This is due to management's insistent search for possible cost reductions in every part of the manufacturing concern.

FACILITY SYSTEM

The facility system provides plant, equipment, tools, power, and utilities, as well as essential services such as maintenance, which are required to make the product. The objective of the facility system is to see that the facilities and services are available to permit production at a desirable cost level, quality standard, and volume.

This system is usually comprised of subsystems which are operated by the plant engineering department (which may include the maintenance department) or its less obvious partner—the finance department. Of course, the latter arranges for, or provides the money, while the former transforms it into equipment and services.

Finance

Although the first-line supervisor has little direct contact with the finance department, he has a discernible impact on the decisions made by the department. The finance department, of course, is responsible for securing capital to provide facilities and the equipment to operate. Even under the most favorable circumstances, this aim is not an easy task. The financial managers find bankers almost as difficult to work with as foremen find union committeemen.

However, it must be recognized that the performance of the workers in a foreman's department affects profit which has an important influence on the financial position of the company. Less direct, but equally important, is the performance of the foreman in meeting quality specifications and delivery promises. These accomplishments contribute to the reputation of the firm and establish, in the economic community, the potential for the company to grow and prosper in a highly competitive environment.

Plant Engineering

Because of his daily contact with plant engineering the foreman readily recognizes how this important activity helps him to meet his production, cost, and quality commitments. Although there occasionally appears to be little visible semblance of "system" in the operation of the maintenance department, closer examination will show that maintenance people have two major functions between which they must allocate their time.

Most maintenance departments are actively involved in continuing efforts to expand, improve, and upgrade plant facilities. In many companies the foremen make substantial contributions to the determination of needs, the formulation of plans, and the layout of departments. In many cases they have an equally important part in the planning and layout of new and expanded facilities.

The second major aspect of the plant engineering department is the maintenance of facilities for on-going operations. Because of the close relationship between the production and maintenance departments, it has been customary over the years to rely largely on verbal communications. Lately, however, it has become increasingly common for the maintenance operation to document and plan assignments, control performance of maintenance labor, and allocate the cost of maintenance to appropriate cost centers. This change has resulted in an additional system structure within maintenance, which complicates the requests and authorizations initiated by the foreman.

The foreman has an important role in maintenance. Particularly in the processing industries, he must anticipate equipment breakdowns in order to avoid expensive shutdowns. In addition, his suggestions can significantly improve the life of equipment and reduce the cost of maintenance.

Perhaps the most important function of the foreman in this area is instructing, motivating, and monitoring the activities of his workers to be sure that they are familiar with their equipment, know how to use it, and maintain it in top working order. He should make sure that they receive help when they report equipment problems. It is readily recognized among manufacturing people that the attitude of the worker towards the maintenance of his equipment appears to vary in direct proportion to the interest and response of the foreman, and the rapidity with which the maintenance department responds when difficulties are reported.

Many production employees develop an attachment to the equipment that they operate and if given the opportunity will take pride in maintaining it at peak operating efficiency. Behavior of workers in this respect reflects the interest of the foreman and the maintenance department in keeping all equipment in first-class operating condition.

ENVIRONMENTAL SYSTEMS

The environmental systems are those systems and subsystems intended to create and maintain a satisfactory environment both for the workers and for the community in which the enterprise is located. These systems have as their immediate objective the elimination of health hazards, both inside and outside of the plant. Their long-range objective is to create and maintain an environment in which both workers and the outside community can be safe and comfortable.

Working Environment

A major portion of the effort to maintain a good working environment is usually centered around the safety engineer and the safety committees which operate to prevent accidents and lost time. In larger companies, and in many smaller ones, the safety system is quite elaborate with procedures and disciplines designed to maintain a high degree of interest in safety and to anticipate and prevent accidents.

The foreman today finds himself pressured by his workers as well as by his management to maintain high standards of physical comfort and safety. Some old-time foremen feel that this is an indication of softness in the modern generation. Nothing could be further from reality. Regardless of its humanitarian aspects, which are not of minor importance, maintaining a healthy and safe environment contributes to the economic welfare of the corporation and can materially affect the performance of the workers from the standpoint of productivity and quality. The perceptive foreman recognizes his responsibility in these areas.

Perhaps the most discouraging aspect of the foreman's role in this area is the fact that he finds himself constantly reminding his workers to abide by safety rules and regulations. It is perhaps necessary to recognize that it takes many years of constant effort to develop habits which will be self-enforced. It takes more than setting a good example to achieve 100 percent compliance with safety rules and regulations. It is necessary that safety practices be periodically reviewed from the standpoint of their contribution to the safety of the worker. When some safety practices are found to be unnecessary it does not mean that all safety warnings are suspect. Rather it limits their observance to critical areas. A positive attitude towards these rules on the part of the foreman can do much to make safety an accepted and continuing interest and concern of operating employees.

The maintenance department is continually concerned with providing the best in light, heat, and ventilation. These objectives are accomplished through preventive maintenance programs designed, in part, to maintain optimum working conditions.

Community Environment

Although it may be stretching a point, we include community relations in the environmental system because they are a part of the total climate in which the enterprise operates. Companies usually have two highly structured programs which are designed, first to improve and maintain public relations, and second, to contribute to community welfare and development.

Today there is a ground swell of interest in the role of the industrial enterprise in the improvement and development of the community in which it is located. Outside the plant there is concern with discharge of pollutants into the air or water, and the creation of noise which detracts from the quality of surrounding neighborhoods. In recent years, many companies have designed and built plants which enhanced rather than degraded the neighborhood.

For many years, owners and top management of businesses have felt it their responsibility to participate in community affairs. They were active on hospital boards, United Fund Drives, Service Club activities, and church and fraternal organizations. More recently, however, it has become increasingly clear that this social participation is not sufficient. Today it is recognized that genuine participation by all the key members of management in community affairs is necessary. Therefore, today, much more interest is taken in encouraging members of management to take a significant part in promoting the community's best interests.

Perhaps no aspect of the foreman's responsibility is more overlooked than the contribution he can make to public and community relations. As a matter of fact it is difficult for the foreman to avoid communicating an image of his company to the community, since usually it is well known that he is a supervisor at a particular company. Many foremen neglect to take advantage of opportunities to enhance the image of their employer, while others fail to recognize that their participation in community affairs is important in terms of their personal development. Of course participation in community affairs will not guarantee advancement. However, when two equally competent supervisors are being considered for promotion this factor could tip the balance in one's favor.

SUMMARY

In this chapter we have attempted to take a new approach to describing the foreman's job by considering it in terms of the systems concept. Most of the systems designed to make an enterprise operate effectively converge at the foreman's level. We have said that the foreman is the catalyst which effects a union of the resources made available by these systems. For many of these systems, he provides the essential link which makes the systems interface and function as a coordinated whole.

In short, his job is to see that the workers provided to him by the personnel system, the materials provided him by the production system, and the equipment provided by the facilities system are put together in such a way as to satisfy the quality and cost constraints. This achievement is of no small order. It means that all of the functions which the foreman has to perform in implementing these systems must be effectively carried out. If all systems are functioning properly, he will be within his cost estimates. However, he must be constantly alert to the possibility of any one of these resources not being up to par, of breakdowns in the systems, and a thousand and one other failures of man or machine which can, if not anticipated and prevented, prevent his people from producing as they are able to do.

Chapter 5

Human Relations:
The Foreman in His
Personnel Management Role

The first-line supervisor acts as a link between upper management and company employees. Policies, procedures and direction, the requirements of profit or production, and the overall goals of the firm are met through the efforts and competence of the foreman. Management action, to be successful, must take place within a framework called the organization. The most important part of an organized system is people. The major responsibility of a supervisor is to deal with people so they can contribute their best efforts to meet the needs of the organization.

At this point a distinction between supervising and managing should be made. To supervise, in the strict sense of the word, means to over-see or look after. Managing—using supervision as a form of control, allied with other factors such as motivation, coordination, and direction—is used to control and attain the objectives of the organization through people. Along with technological progress in industry, management techniques have also improved. The development of management, however, has not been as fast, nor has it gone as far, as the development of technology.

During the Industrial Revolution, supervision was mainly used to control machines and technical problems. People were secondary elements in this organization system, and administration procedures were simple. With increased complexity in the industrial environment due to an increase in machinery costs and the need for more output, interest in the problems of management increased.

In the early part of this century, Frederick Taylor developed what he called "the principles of scientific management." Basically, Taylor's thesis was that people's efforts could be maximized through the application of more systematic supervisory techniques. In Taylor's time, these principles were well received. Their use improved the quality of first-line management, resulting in improved productivity in the many companies which used them.

The next step in management thought was the human relations or "people orientation" of the 1940s. With this movement came the advent of fringe benefits and the improvement of job conditions. Now people were starting to take a different place in the management framework.

Since the late 1950s it has been increasingly recognized that the human relations approach and the motivational sciences in general can make contributions to productivity and aid in the accomplishment of organizational goals. The importance of two-way communication, for example, has been recognized. Today, in the presently existing social climate, the foreman must be more and more concerned with the human relations aspects of this job. In most instances a good knowledge of human relations is more important than technical knowledge.[1]

MANAGEMENT STYLES

The way in which a first-line supervisor relates to the employees under his direction may be called his "management style." Management styles vary from one person to another, from one situation to another, and from one subordinate to another. Graphically this may be represented as shown in Fig. 5-1.

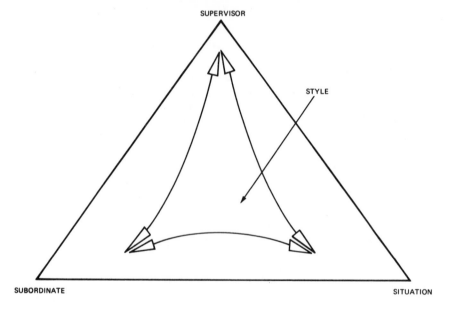

Fig. 5-1 The interrelationships of the supervisor and his style upon his subordinates and the situation.

The same supervisor may use a different style when confronted with a new situation, or he may elect to employ a different style from his usual one in working with different employees. The same supervisor may have several different approaches, allowing the context to determine which one is most appropriate.

To suggest that all foremen should develop one management style in preference to all others would imply that only one style is effective. Each style is relatively effective depending on the philosophy of top management and other factors. For example, an authoritarian style adopted by a foreman in a "laissez-faire" environment would cause

---

1. A good summary of the development of management thought is given in Claude S. George, Jr., *The History of Management Thought* (Prentice-Hall, Inc.: Englewood Cliffs, N.J., 1968).

continuous friction between the foreman and upper management. What we will do is to briefly describe several distinct management styles; ultimately it is up to the individual to evaluate these styles in relation to the environment within which he operates.

For simplicity, management styles may be grouped into three broad categories; the taskmaster or "authoritarian leader" style, the laissez-faire or "don't rock the boat" style, and the influential leader style. Each of these are discussed below.

Taskmaster

Typically the taskmaster directs or commands. He does not permit subordinates to question his orders or to take independent action. He exhibits little or no consideration for people or their problems. Decisions, right or wrong, good or bad, are railroaded through. He achieves production objectives as long as he is present and can observe, control, and direct all activities. He must constantly supervise. His only influence is his formal authority. His employees exhibit minimal effort. In contrast he must exercise maximum effort to meet management's production objectives. He is production oriented rather than people oriented. In the absence of a union, employee complaints will not surface though in due time employees may seek relief by organizing. Operating in a union environment, employee complaints surface through union channels in the form of written grievances.

Laissez-Faire

At the opposite extreme from the taskmaster type of supervisor is the "laissez-faire" type. Production requirements would be nice to accomplish providing people will make the effort. He listens to employee complaints and may or may not act on them. He maintains a relatively complaint-free department by abdicating his role as a manager. He tends to identify with the employee group rather than with management. Consciously or unconsciously he wishes to remain "one of the boys" rather than being their leader.

Influential Leadership

This style of management is personified by the successful merging of both formal and informal leadership. Employees know who is "running the show" yet they do their jobs because they want to. The leader clearly identifies with management goals and objectives and simultaneously is empathetic toward employees. He has confidence in his own ability and has confidence and trust in his employees. He expects that most employees will meet his standards, and he deals effectively and promptly with the occasional one who does not. He listens to his employees, but he makes the final decisions. Typically he meets or exceeds management's objectives. He does this with relatively few employee complaints, and the few received are handled promptly and fairly. If there is a union he respects it and has the respect of union representatives. As a consequence few written grievances are filed.

It is this concept of leadership to which most managements subscribe. It is a style that can only be developed if management believes in and lives by the philosophy that most, if not all, people want to do their best.

The supervisor using this style requires that all employees working under him contribute to the organization. It is difficult to be an influential leader. The influential leader style requires a great deal of work and will test the talents and patience of the supervisor who wishes to use this in achieving his goals. The results are long lasting, however, mainly because of the foreman's reliance upon the basic fact that all people have a need for personal accomplishment.

A foreman who wants to be an influential leader need not possess supernatural abilities, nor does he need to impress his employees. To exercise his influence he should, on the contrary, strive to be "down to earth" in his relationships. He should be confident of his own abilities, and he needs to be able to trust people. He must learn to make decisions, but he also needs to know how to delegate work and follow up to see that the work has been accomplished. An influential leader must be a "self-starter" if he is to motivate others. Perhaps not every foreman is disposed to exercise this type of leadership, but there is little doubt that in the long run supervision based on the principles of influence rather than coercion is most effective.

THE MANAGEMENT PROCESS

Regardless of his management style, every foreman must accomplish objectives through the employees he supervises. The foreman's role is one of motivating his employees, controlling their efforts, and using his authority to achieve production goals. These items, taken as a whole, can be called the management process.

Motivation

At times the foreman must encourage employees to do the work assigned to them in improved fashion. At other times he must motivate his employees simply in order to achieve present levels of performance. He must at other times assist his employees in adjusting to changes that are occurring within the organization and within the department.

The foreman then is faced with motivating others. How can this be done? Research in the social sciences reveals that the process of motivation is not simple. Motivation has to do with providing the employee with the desire for progress and development. In part, motivation is encouraged by fair wages and fringe benefits, good working conditions, and opportunities for advancement. Some of the elements necessary for motivated employees are beyond the foreman's control. Pay, for example, is not normally established by the foreman. However, he can recognize superior performance, he can attempt to understand the employee's viewpoint, and he can represent employees to higher management.

As a minimum, the foreman should recognize the importance of motivation in his work force, and should anticipate the effects of his own actions upon the motivational level of his department. Also, he should try to view the larger organization through the eyes of his employees and again seek to anticipate the effects of company policies and actions upon them. The foreman should realize that a negative approach is seldom effective in improving motivation. The use of threats, for example, is more likely to cause the employee to retaliate than to improve. Retaliation may range from quitting to slowdowns, grievances, or even sabotage.

In contrast, positive techniques such as recognition and mutual goal setting are almost always effective, at least to some degree, in improving motivation. By recognizing the efforts his employees are making the foreman can encourage each individual to improve his performance. The recognition technique can be used even when performance is below standard. Instead of showing displeasure at the employee's substandard work, you recognize that the man is trying. By recognizing that he is doing his best, you provide him with a positive experience, and this encourages him to learn the job properly and to strive for better results.

A second powerful motivational tool the supervisor should develop is skill in using goal setting techniques. Goal setting in combination with progressive recognition will accomplish the desired company objective. In goal setting the supervisor should keep in mind that the goal should be attainable in terms of the individual or group's capability. At the same time, each goal should be sufficiently difficult to challenge those involved. To effectively use goal setting as a motivational tool, progress toward goals must be measured, and regardless of how small the increment, must be rewarded in the form of recognized accomplishment. By measuring progress toward goals the necessary controls are established to take corrective action and meet management objectives. When progress is too slow the supervisor should solicit the subordinate's suggestions to eliminate the problems impeding progress. This is again a form of recognition. In this atmosphere employees will generally volunteer suggestions for improvement.

Control

To accomplish departmental and company objectives, the foreman must control the efforts of his employees. According to one widely used management textbook, "The aim of control is to make sure that the results of operations conform as closely as possible to established goals."[2] The foreman is normally provided with a specific set of goals. In order to meet these goals he makes work assignments, schedules the efforts of his employees, and follows up to see that each employee is performing satisfactorily. When the foreman checks to see that work is proceeding according to plan, he is engaged in control. Control is a very important aspect of first-line management. If the foreman fails to check on his employees, they are likely to feel there is little urgency attached to the job to which they have been assigned. This type of attitude will quickly lead to job delays, and the foreman is likely to find that the department is failing to reach its goals.

According to Newman, Summer, and Warren,[3] the control process contains three essential elements:

1) *Standards that represent desired performance.* Everyone should be aware of the performance expected of him; he should know what final results are desired.
2) *A comparison of actual results against the standards.* The foreman who has established a standard of performance can use this standard as a model with which to compare actual performance.
3) *Corrective action.* When job performance falls below the established standard the foreman must take action to improve performance and bring it into line with the standard.

Authority

Another concept that is important for the foreman is that of authority. Authority may be thought of as the right to make requests or to give instructions necessary to achieve established objectives. It is useful to distinguish between formal and informal authority. Formal authority can be defined as the foreman's right to issue orders and instructions because of his appointed position in the organization as a manager. Formal authority, in

---

2. William H. Newman, Charles E. Summer, and E. Kirby Warren, *The Process of Management,* 2nd ed. (Prentice-Hall, Inc.: Englewood Cliffs, N.J., 1967), 675.

3. *Ibid.*

other words, is bestowed upon him by the organization. Thus one cannot possess formal authority unless he has been promoted to a position of responsibility within the company.

Informal authority, on the other hand, is the authority that a person holds because of the respect that others have for him. This type of authority cannot be assigned to a foreman simply by means of promotion; it must be earned by the way the foreman carries out his job.

In an earlier book published in this series the following paragraph discussed authority:

> Like other tools, authority can be used expertly or clumsily. And like other tools, it must be used by men. Top managers have long since unhappily recognized that the delegation of considerable authority to middle and lower management is no guarantee of effective management. Indeed, some managers seem to supervise better with less authority than with more. And, conversely, some supervisors function better with more of it than less. The issue is not only how much authority but how it is used and by whom.[4]

The points made are valid. One of the foreman's most important tasks is to learn how to use the authority delegated to him. Of equal, and perhaps greater importance, he must earn informal authority by dealing fairly with the men he supervises.

This last point cannot be overemphasized. To be successful the first-line supervisor must earn the right to manage by earning the respect of his employees. The fact that he is vested with management authority provides him only with the opportunity to earn this respect. Vested authority alone will not assure productive results.

Furthermore, each foreman must develop his own unique leadership style in order to achieve this informal authority, or right of leadership. He cannot simply copy the patterns of leadership used by some other foreman or by his own supervisor. How can this be done? *First,* the foreman must subscribe wholeheartedly to company objectives. He represents the company to his employees, and he will not achieve their respect if he makes light of company goals and purposes. *Second,* the foreman must deal fairly with each employee. To provide an example, the foreman should make every effort to see that work loads are evenly divided among the members of his department. *Third,* the foreman should know the jobs in his department. It is very difficult to gain employee respect if you yourself do not know how to perform the job you ask others to do. *Fourth,* the foreman should interpret company policies and actions to his employees. If a change is to be made that affects his department, the foreman is the one who should break the news and explain how such a change will affect each member of the department. *Fifth,* the foreman must be sincerely interested in his employees. In addition, he should choose appropriate ways to convey his feeling, as for example, remembering to inquire about a man's family if there has been a recent illness.

These five points are only suggestions, and certainly the list is not exhaustive. As a foreman you should be able to think of many others.

Goals

The foreman motivates his employees, controls their efforts, and uses his authority in order to accomplish goals. In other words, the management process as we have defined it is *goal directed.* A supervisor who operates his department on a day-to-day basis, with-

---

4. Ivan R. Vernon, ed., *Organization for Manufacturing* (Society of Manufacturing Engineers: Dearborn, Mich., 1970), 33.

out keeping his eye on the company's ultimate objectives, is wasting his time and the company's time and money. Decisions made today directly affect those to be made tomorrow and next week and next month. It is only by managing in a goal-directed fashion that the foreman can assure that the decisions he makes today will work out well in the future.

Two kinds of goals can be defined. First, there are the broad company goals that all members of the organization should be working to achieve. Cost reduction is an example of this kind of goal. The second type of goal is the operational goal. Operational goals must be established within each department in order to achieve the overall company goals. To achieve the overall company goal of cost reduction, the foreman might establish the operational goals of reducing scrap and rework by 50 percent during the next month.

Overall goals and operational goals must be coordinated. In establishing the operational goals for his department, the foreman first studies the overall goals. Next he examines his own department to determine what he can do to help meet company goals. Then he expresses in exact terms what the operational goal is and how and when it will be achieved.

Goals established for the department should be realistic and attainable. If goals are set too far above what can be realistically achieved, discouragement may set in and everyone involved will tend to disregard them. One good way to ensure that proper goals are established is by using the mutual goal setting technique discussed earlier. In addition to improving motivation, mutual goal setting is a way of establishing the correct goals. By setting goals in consultation with departmental employees, the foreman gets the benefit of the expertise of each individual.

THE EMPLOYEE—THE FOREMAN'S FOCUS

The foreman's most important job is to obtain the best efforts of his employees. The first-line supervisor's ultimate success is directly related to the way in which he is able to interact with the members of his department. The successful foreman quickly learns that people are individuals and must be handled differently. Important differences exist in sex, education, age, experience, and personality. In this section we take a look at the employees the foreman supervises and examine some of these differences.

Sex

According to one authority,[5] the composition of the labor force in 1960 was 32.2 percent female and 67.8 percent male. The trend is towards an increasing number of women in the work force, and it is estimated that by 1980 35.9 percent of the work force will be female. This would represent an 11.5 percent increase in a period of only twenty years.

There are several reasons for this increase. First, there has been an increase in the female-male birth ratio during recent years. Second, the trend toward cleaner and less tiring jobs in industry is attracting more women than has been true in past years. A third reason is that there is an increased tendency for males to complete courses of study leading to high-paying technical and professional positions, thus vacating jobs requiring less academic preparation.

---

5. D. F. Johnston, "Educational Attainment of Workers, March, 1964," *Monthly Labor Review*, Vol. 88, No. 5 (May, 1965), 519.

Although several industries (textiles and electronics, for example) have long had a high proportion of women workers, many foremen in other industries have had no experience in supervising females. This is a situation that is likely to change in the near future.

Education

Studies also indicate that the educational level of the average industrial worker is increasing steadily. While few individuals who have completed four years of college will seek industrial jobs at the operating level, it is probable that the foreman will be supervising employees with some college experience. Foremen must be prepared to recognize and adjust to the sociological changes created by progressive educational norms.

Highly educated individuals tend to react differently in work situations, and supervisors will need to take into account the different needs of such employees. It is worth noting also that higher educational levels are one of the main forces behind the human relations approach to management. Better educated employees are more apt to have their own ideas about how to accomplish a particular task, and they have fewer reservations about expressing their opinions. By the same token, these persons are better prepared to make positive contributions to the achievement of company and departmental goals.

Age and Experience

The age span of industrial employees ranges from 18 years to 65 years. In other words, almost a half century may separate the new hire from the ready-to-retire worker. In view of the current generation-gap controversy, it is surprising that this age spread has not created more problems. In most cases, however, older employees do not resent young workers but rather regard them in a fatherly manner. Likewise young employees generally respect their older peers perhaps not because of their age but because of their superior knowledge and experience.

Age differences are worth the foreman's consideration. Potential resentment by older workers of young employees can sometimes be forestalled by assigning the younger person to the old hand for training. The more experienced man is pleased that his experience and skill is recognized, and the younger man normally will not resent taking instructions from his senior. Younger foremen may find this approach especially useful in breaking in new employees close to their own age.

Personality

All of us have our own habits, preferences, likes and dislikes, and even peculiarities. We are entitled to them, and so is the next man. If we think he may have a few more peculiarities than we do, it is good to remember that he may think the same about us!

Realistically, though, we must recognize that some people are more difficult to deal with than others. Negative attitudes and resentment of authority are troublesome, but it is the foreman's job to contend with employees exhibiting these traits. It is best to try to deal with a negative, resentful individual on a friendly basis. Responding to him in a hostile fashion, even though he seems to invite such a response, seldom improves the situation. Dealing with a difficult personality calls for the utmost in self-control, but continued fair treatment and refusal to "take the bait" generally will cause such a person to change his attitude and behavior.

THE FOREMAN AS AN INDIVIDUAL

Like their employees, foremen also differ significantly. There are young foremen and older foremen, college-educated foremen and men promoted from the ranks. Certainly there are many other differences as well, but we have singled out the characteristics of age and education for special consideration since it is these two factors that seem particularly relevant.

The Young Foreman

The ideal supervisor would combine the vigor and enthusiasm of youth with the experience and wisdom that can be acquired only with time. In fact many young foremen do possess considerable experience, and many older men are still enthusiastic and vigorous in outlook. Often, however, young foremen are both lacking in the experience needed to deal with people and short on technical expertise. The older man may be quite versed in the technical aspects of his work and know how to obtain the best efforts of his people, but there are some older supervisors who are lacking in drive and stamina.

The young foreman might be identified as one who is significantly younger than the employees he supervises. There is an increasing tendency in industry today to hire younger foremen. This trend is in part attributable to the fact that young college graduates are being recruited at the entry position of foremen. In other words, some companies use the foreman's position as the initial job for new college graduates instead of reserving it for qualified hourly employees.

In addition, some companies are stressing the opportunity of becoming a foreman to their younger production workers regardless of educational level. One large automobile company, for example, maintains a leadership school especially for production employees who wish to prepare themselves for supervisory positions. The emphasis is upon young employees.

Both the young employee, recently promoted from the ranks, and the young college graduate are likely to encounter certain problems when they begin their tour as a foreman. These problems are frequently more pronounced for the recent college graduate. This individual, thrust into a totally strange, almost alien environment, can expect a certain amount of stress. The young college graduate is sure to be baited. Inevitably, one of the older workers will ask him to requisition a left-handed mallet for a special job. One new foreman was told that he was expected to furnish cookies for the department's coffee break on Fridays!

During his first few weeks on the job, the young supervisor—college man or not—faces the same problems that any other supervisor would in going into a new work area—new people, new machinery, new parts, new service contacts, etc. But in addition to these, he has to earn the confidence and respect of his subordinates. This is not an easy task. It pays him to refrain (even more so now than later) from adopting an authoritarian air. A straightforward "I don't know, but I'll find out," and a reliance on the experience of those who have been around a long while works better than any bluff ever will. Nothing obtained from a college education pays handsomer dividends than just the perseverance to get through—perseverance which applied to a foreman's job turns into drive, zeal, and satisfaction in a job well done.

What an employee who is promoted to foreman may lack in education (mathamatics, sociology, psychology, engineering, mechanics, etc.) he usually makes up in experience. He has been around his subordinates (or others like them) for a while, and knows how they think and act. He has observed and "served" various managerial styles, and has a good feeling for what kind of directives get things done—and which *don't*. He has empathy for the man running the machine, or the man on the assembly line. He realizes the monotony and drudgery associated with some of these jobs. The difficulties that a promoted young foreman faces are similar to those of the college graduate. He now has to give orders to his former "buddies," orders which he might have taken only weeks before. There might even be resentment of him from the others, or even jealousy if there was competition for the position.

In summary, it's a rough road to follow. Personality adjustments and attitude changes may have to be made. The success of the operation rests on the young supervisor's ability and flexibility—and his desire to do a good job.

The Foreman's Attitude

All the education and technical expertise in the world is not enough for a foreman who doesn't know how to get along with people. The poorest foreman is one whose personality is such that he himself creates friction, hostility, and opposition. Any foreman must watch his own attitude and behavior very carefully. He should always respect those who work for him, and must never by word or deed demonstrate that he believes the members of his work force are somehow inferior to him.

Supervision by its very nature requires the exercise of authority. Authority must be exercised very carefully, however. Subordinates who harbor negative attitudes toward authority figures need very little prompting to begin criticizing a foreman as dictatorial in an effort to lessen his effectiveness.

The foreman's attitude should be one of impartiality. One member of the work group must never be favored over another. This is especially important with regard to members of minority groups. A black foreman, for example, should be very careful not to appear to favor those of his own race, nor conversely should a white supervisor permit it to appear that he favors the white men over the black men who are working for him.

The foreman needs to recognize the informal groups that inevitably spring up and maintain a positive attitude towards them. He may, for instance, find that within his department there are two or more distinct groupings of individuals who prefer to work and socialize with each other. This is quite normal and to be expected. His attitude toward such groups should be positive rather than negative. By recognizing and giving support to such groups he can gain their respect and their support in attaining company and departmental objectives.

THE FOREMAN'S ROLE IN LABOR RELATIONS

In those shops where employees are represented by a union, the supervisor has an additional opportunity to develop skill in applying the techniques of recognition and goal setting in his relationships with union representatives. He should view the goal of the union representative as that of representing his constituents. The supervisor should keep clearly in mind the fact that the union representative's need for recognition is greater than that of the average person and is partially satisfied by his election to office. The supervisor who can help the union representative satisfy this need for recognition will establish a highly satisfactory and productive working environment. He can accomplish this by recognizing and meeting the legitimate needs of his employees before they take the form of demands which must be presented as formal grievances by the union representative.

In so conducting himself the supervisor is not "selling the company short." He is simply recognizing the union representative's right to exist rather than thoughtlessly creating opportunities for confrontation. To work successfully with the union the proper environment must be established by upper management. For example, the introductory paragraphs of The National Agreement between the U.A.W. and General Motors provide a suitable environment for such a relationship. These paragraphs read:

> The management of General Motors recognizes that it cannot get along without labor any more than labor can get along without the management. Both are in the same business and the success of that business is vital to all concerned. This requires that both management and the employees work together to the end that the quality and cost of the product will prove increasingly satisfactory and attractive so that the business will be continuously successful.
>
> General Motors holds that the basic interests of employers and employees are the same. However, at times employees and the management have different ideas on various matters affecting their relationship. The management of General Motors is convinced that there is no reason why these differences cannot be peacefully and satisfactorily adjusted by sincere and patient effort on both sides.

The key to good labor relations does not differ from the key to good human relations. The late James E. Goodman stated the principle succinctly in the film "New Era for Management".

The answer to a harmonious relationship with our employees is pure and simple. It's written in the Golden Rule. No matter how trite it seems, when we do unto others as we expect them to do unto us we are paid back many fold.

To achieve rapport with his people and maintain a harmonious relationship between employees and himself the foreman must often place himself in the employee's position and consider if this is the way he would like to be treated. How the foreman handles his employees every day, on a continuing basis, determines their attitude toward their job, their supervisor, and the company and, in turn, their productivity.

Studies indicate that 85 percent of all employees never cause any problems. This then, leaves 15 percent who need some type of corrective action. With this small minority the foreman must have some means of improving or correcting the employee or he must resort to disciplinary action. Disciplinary action—oral or written warnings, time off, or discharge—should only be used when all other reasonable efforts by the foreman have failed to bring about satisfactory results. Outside of extreme violations, i.e., fighting, destructive acts, misappropriation of company property, etc., the offender may indicate by some type of warning signs that he is drifting into an abnormal behavior pattern. The foreman who knows his people will be aware of these signals, and when they appear he should have an informal discussion with the employee before the condition goes too far.

Some of these signs may be that the man is reporting late for work or is beginning to build up an absentee record. His work in either or both quantity or quality may be falling off. His attitude may be changing negatively. An informal discussion may disclose that the foreman is contributing to the employee's actions, i.e., that the employee had not been instructed on the importance of his attendance; or that the importance of quality has never been explained fully. A change of attitude may have resulted from some request he made of the foreman to which he has never been given a reply.

If the informal discussion does not lead to improvement, a second discussion is in order. The employee should not be threatened. Instead the foreman's approach should be one of "What can I do to help you improve?" The discussion might include a review of

EMPLOYEE DISCIPLINARY NOTICE

Date _____

Employee's Name: _____   Dept.-Clk. No. _____

Offense: _____

Details: _____
_____
_____
_____

Disciplinary action taken: ☐ Verbal warning,   ☐ Written warning,
                            ☐ Time off penalty of _____days.

Other action and comments: _____
_____

Management witnesses: _____

Union witnesses: _____

Copies to: Employee
            Department File   Supervisor's Signature_____
            Industrial Relations

Fig. 5–2 Employee disciplinary notice used by foreman in a large manufacturing company. One copy is given to the employee, one is retained in the departmental files, and the third is forwarded to the industrial relations department.

the employee's past performance, with emphasis on positive rather than negative aspects. The session should be a means of "getting to" the employee, not "getting at" him.

Disciplinary measures are sometimes necessary, and normally these are specified in the labor contract. As a rule formal disciplinary measures include written warning slips (see Fig. 5-2), written reprimands, time off without pay, and finally discharge. Before this sequence of formal measures is begun, the foreman should exhaust all the informal means available to him, and before he issues even a written warning slip he should be very sure of his case.

At this stage of formal disciplinary action, the foreman will realize the importance of being on good terms with union representatives. If union leaders regard the foreman as fair they are less likely to give strong support to a union member who has become a disciplinary problem. If the union representative is on good terms with the foreman and respects him he may even help in counseling the employee to assist him in performing his job in accordance with company requirements.

The human factor is an integral part of the supervisor's job. Employees who respect their foreman for his openmindedness and fair dealings will not resort to making trouble or writing grievances to attain an equitable settlement of their complaints. A willingness to work on a man-to-man basis with employees will go far in helping the foreman to achieve good labor relations.

To expand on these thoughts for a moment the successful supervisor, when faced with an employee problem, does not immediately categorize it as real or imaginary. He attempts to place himself in the employee's position in an effort to understand. He evaluates the fairness of the request and takes action in the form of a commitment or a denial of the request, and when the request is denied he explains his reasons.

The supervisor when faced with an employee problem that could be the basis for disciplinary action under existing plant rules has a responsibility to himself, and more importantly to the employee, to try to understand the reason for deviation. He must relate the deviation to his knowledge of the employee's past behavior and attitudes. He should make certain, whether there is a union or not, that the employee understands the rule and the need for the rule and attempt to counsel him. Depending on the seriousness of the violation, he may or may not dispense formal discipline. The supervisor in some situations will have no choice but to take immediate formal action to protect other employees, company property, or even the individual himself from harm.

In most situations, however, there is time for the supervisor to consider the individual's past performance, work history, and attitudes as reflected in past behavior and to determine if possible whether he, some other member of the group, management, or some unrelated work situation gave rise to the deviation from acceptable behavior. Frequently he may find it desirable to seek help in arriving at his decision by reviewing the facts and background with a superior. In most cases a discussion with the employee, explaining the reason why the employee's behavior or action is not acceptable, will suffice to avoid future problems. In those situations where the employee does not respond, refuses to accept management's position, or repeats the unacceptable behavior a more formal approach to corrective discipline should be used.

Taking a punitive disciplinary approach at the first instance of unacceptable behavior, except where persons or property are involved, will only lead to excessive grievances and poor employee attitudes. The employee group will not respond favorably and company objectives are not apt to be met.

If under stress the supervisor can keep in mind that his major responsibility is to help people develop and be more productive for their own personal gain and benefit, he will take time to "cool it" before taking action. To the extent that he demonstrates sincere concern for his employees he will be successful in dealing with the union. The supervisor using this approach will have few formal grievances or complaints brought to the attention of the union and will have far more time to handle his other job responsibilities. It is the personal attitude of the supervisor reflected in his every-day behavior that will determine in the final analysis how far he will advance in the management organization.

In closing it would be well to keep in mind a statement by Burt K. Scanlan: "A supervisor with a certain degree of personnelmindedness will tend to achieve greater efficiency and effectiveness than one who is solely production oriented."[6] For many individuals who have been involved in manufacturing for the larger part of their adult lives, this human relations awareness may seem to be cryptic and grandiose.

But industry is changing drastically. So are the people in it. Old systems and procedures must make way for new ones. People's attitudes, needs, and desires change. The concepts with which we supervise our people must be flexible enough to be remolded as the need arises.

---

6. Burt K. Scanlan, "Increasing Supervisory Effectiveness through Personnel Management," *Personnel Management*, Vol. 27, No. 5 (Sept.–Oct., 1964), 24–27.

Chapter 6

Orientation and Training

One of the foreman's most important responsibilities is orienting and training the employees he supervises. Proper training of those workers assigned to his department is the foreman's best guarantee of maintaining a group of workers who are able and willing to work to achieve established objectives.

In this chapter we consider these activities from the foreman's viewpoint. The first topic covered is that of responsibility. Who is responsible for seeing that proper orientation and training policies are formulated? Who is responsible for implementing these policies? Where does the foreman fit in?

Next we examine the approaches and techniques used for introducing new employees into the work group. What are the "tricks of the trade?" More accurately, what are the proven orientation techniques that a foreman may use to see that new workers start off on the right foot?

Finally, this chapter discusses the principles and techniques of job training. Here the effort is to show how the foreman may train his work force, with the varying backgrounds of its individual members, to function effectively as a unit to achieve departmental goals.

RESPONSIBILITY FOR ORIENTATION AND TRAINING

The responsibility for orienting and training employees rests with several people. First of all, it is the foreman's responsibility. Secondly, it is a man's own responsibility to improve and develop himself so he is able to do his job. Third, the foreman's immediate supervisor (a general foreman or superintendent) has a responsibility to see that training is done effectively in departments under his supervision. And finally, the staff department—personnel or training—has a responsibility to see that employees are properly trained in the specific departments in which they work. Let us consider each of these in some detail.

The Foreman's Responsibility

First of all, the foreman is responsible for his own training and development. He should be an effective manager of his own department and thereby set an example for his people. He should keep his managerial skills up to date and should stay abreast of the technology in his field. He should participate in training programs conducted in his plant and outside of the plant. He should read selected articles and books. He should actively participate in appropriate management clubs and professional groups. And he should be actively involved in other activities, such as a Toastmaster Club, Rotary Club, or United Fund, that will help him be a more effective leader. All this activity has to be conducted in such a way as not to interfere with his family responsibilities.

The foreman has prime responsibility for the effective performance of employees working in his department. Therefore, he is responsible for orienting and training employees so that they are prepared to do their jobs effectively. This training responsibility includes all new employees, all transferred employees, and all employees currently working in the department. The foreman is responsible for the continuous training of his people to do the jobs that they are assigned; when new jobs are assigned, he should see that new training is given.

It is important to differentiate between the responsibility for training and the training itself. The first-line supervisor may not train his employees directly, but it is his responsibility for seeing that training is done effectively. He must take an active part in training, but he may call on both his experienced employees and other departments for assistance.

The Employee's Responsibility

Each individual in industry, whether he is an hourly employee or a top-level manager, has a responsibility for his own training and development. At the operating level, this is not so true as at higher levels of management. However, workers must be concerned about their own training. For example, if a worker does not feel that he can perform his job properly because of inadequate training, he should convey this to his foreman. The foreman may arrange for additional training, or suggest outside courses. In any case the employee has indicated he is not satisfied with his progress, and wants to do something to improve it.

Responsibility of the General Foreman or Superintendent

The foreman's immediate supervisor also has an important responsibility in the training of employees. Middle-level managers are responsible for the productivity and efficiency of the departments they supervise. Therefore, they are also responsible for seeing that the foreman in each department is doing an effective job of training. That a middle manager has this responsibility does not mean that he must participate in training activities himself. But it does imply that he should know what kinds of training programs are being conducted. He should be prepared to assist, and he needs to stimulate his foreman to set up and administer such programs.

Responsibility of Outside Departments

Obviously a "training department" has a degree of responsibility for the training that takes place in the organization. This is also true if a personnel manager has training as one of the functions for which he is responsible. The responsibility of these departments is to stimulate, to encourage, and to assist wherever possible to see that training is effective. They do not have any direct line of authority over the foreman or the workers who come into a department. However, they have a staff responsibility to see that training is done effectively in all departments. If training is poor or nonexistent in a particular department, and the foreman refuses help, they should advise higher management.

Responsibility of the Organization

In addition to the specific responsibilities described above, the organization itself, through its top management and through its policies and procedures, has a responsibility to encourage training and development at all levels of the organization. Therefore, it should make provisions to assist employees with tuition for courses they take independently and should encourage attendance at outside seminars. Very few foremen in industry have had formal training in "how to train new employees." Obviously a foreman cannot be expected to train his employees effectively unless he himself knows how to do the various jobs. The organization should set up programs to ensure that first-line supervisors understand their responsibility for training.

In a large organization it is a good idea to establish a training department. Such a department, in addition to offering in-plant courses, formulates policy and establishes procedures with regard to the training of employees. Even in a small organization it makes sense to make training an extra assignment on the part of some individual at the middle management level. This pinpointing of responsibility can help to close the gap that often exists between company intentions and actual practices in the area of training.

ORIENTATION OF NEW EMPLOYEES

Orientation is the bringing of a new employee into the organization. Implicit in our discussion is the assumption that a new employee who receives a full explanation of the organization, its purposes, policies, objectives, employee benefit programs, and so on, will be more comfortable and thus better prepared to function properly in his new job. Orientation does not cover the teaching of a new job, which is discussed later.

In designing an orientation program, two questions are worth asking:

1) What does the new employee want to know?
2) What does the company want him to know?

The answers to these two questions sometimes are about the same; at other times they vary considerably. For example, a new employee is vitally concerned with the advantages there are in working for the organization. On the other hand, company management is concerned that the new employee understands what is expected of him.

In planning an orientation program, the *subject content* should first of all be determined—what should new employees know in order to become productive and develop positive attitudes toward the company? The second consideration in planning for the orientation and induction of new and transferred employees is to decide *who* will actually cover the items that need to be discussed. Some of them can be most effectively covered by the employment and/or personnel department. People in these departments are generally better acquainted with such items as fringe benefits, insurance programs, pension programs, vacation policies, company products, company history, and so on. The personnel department then might be given responsibility for the segment of the orientation program that covers these items.

There are other topics which can be most effectively covered by the immediate supervisor. These include such things as working hours, department facilities, promotion and job assignment policy, safety rules, introductions to other employees, break periods, and wash up time. This is a typical list that can be expanded upon with little difficulty.

A very unfortunate situation exists in some companies where foremen do not know what topics are being covered by the personnel department and vice versa, with the result that neither the foreman nor the personnel department can possibly do an effective job. This condition exists because a program has not been carefully worked out between the personnel department and line management. There is a solution. Some companies have formed a joint committee of line managers and representatives from the personnel department to plan an orientation program. Their plan includes what is to be covered in the process; who is to do it; when is it to be done; and how it can be done most effectively.

In order to assure an effective job by the foreman as well as the personnel department, check lists should be developed and used. If check lists are not used, the extent and effectiveness of the program depends on the foreman's mood, temperament, and schedule when he receives the new employee, and a poor program is sure to result in many instances.

Sample check lists for three different companies are shown in Figs. 6-1, 6-2, and 6-3. Since these check lists are in actual use, some of them cover special situations that may not exist in some other company. Therefore, if these check lists are used as a model, they should be studied carefully and adapted to fit any new requirements that may exist in your company.

New employees should be given an opportunity to ask questions and to express themselves during the program. There should be a combination of providing information as well as listening. By listening the foreman may learn something about the new employee's past experiences, his ambition and goals, and his personal preferences. People generally talk about those things they consider significant; by listening to what the new employee tells about himself the supervisor is in an excellent position to provide counsel to the employee at a later date.

An effective job of orientation takes more than an oral presentation. Information that is presented orally should be supplemented by means of booklets, visual aids, forms, and other aids which the employee can see as well as hear. Psychologists tell us that a person learns information better if he sees as well as hears a particular message. Care should be taken, particularly in the personnel or training department, to see that effective use is made of visual aids.

In most organizations, the general foreman and superintendent play little if any part in the orientation program. They should be interested in the process and know what is going on both in the personnel department and in the operating department. They should also pay enough attention to see that the job is being done effectively. Sitting in on orientation programs being conducted by the personnel department to see just what is being covered, and to offer suggestions for improvements is advisable. In addition, the general foreman and/or superintendent should take a personal interest in each new employee. For example, at the end of the second week he might sit down with each new employee and formally chat with him. By asking him what questions and what problems the new employee has and finding out how he is getting along he will show his concern. This is the time to uncover poor attitudes, answer any questions, and help resolve any problems that the new employee has. Many companies find out too late—when the employee quits—that a poor job was done in orientation.

In regard to transferred employees, many of the same items should be covered. Obviously, the transferred worker will already be acquainted with many of the company's policies, procedures, rules, and regulations. Therefore, it becomes more important to acquaint him with his new department and his fellow workers.

INDOCTRINATION OF NEW EMPLOYEES

XYZ Company, Detroit, Michigan

Coverage:

All Employees. The intent is to assure new employees of our interest in their welfare and to acquaint them with their rights and responsibilities as employees.

Administration:

It is the responsibility of the supervisor or department head to make certain that each new employee in his department is familiar with the practices and procedures relating to employment.

The supervisor should cover the following with each new employee:

1. Introduce the new employee to fellow workers.
2. Review job duties and acquaint employee with the organization structure.
3. Explain supervisory relationship and that any problems the employee may encounter should be brought to the attention of his supervisor.
4. Inform employee of the company's attitude toward tardiness and absenteeism and explain the procedure for reporting an absence.
5. Instruct employee in the use of the time card.
6. Inform employee of the lunch period and location of cafeteria.
7. Emphasize any other items which you feel will help the employee on his particular job.

The Industrial Relations Department will review the following at the time of hire:

PAY DATA

1. *Pay dates*—Corporate IBM Tab Payroll: every other Friday with one week holdback. Private Payroll: 15th and last day of each month.
2. Shift premium, if applicable.
3. *Cash Advances*—permissible for personal emergencies and are deducted from next paycheck.
4. *Deductions*
   Income tax—Federal and State, if applicable
   Social Security
   Insurance—Aetna and Bankers, if applicable
   Credit Union (issue General Information Sheet)
   U.S. Savings Bonds
   Combined Appeal Plan
5. Pay rate should be kept confidential
6. Overtime permissible only when authorized

HOURS OF WORK

1. Applicable starting and quitting times
2. Lunch period
3. No rest or wash-up period

BENEFITS

1. Holidays
2. Vacation
3. Pay for time absent, if eligible
4. Group insurance (booklet(s) issued)
5. Retirement (booklet issued)

SAFETY

1. First aid facilities and location
2. Report of injury immediately to supervisor

GENERAL

1. Records—notification of change of address, telephone, marital status, etc.
2. Parking
3. Security Pledge, if applicable
4. Employee Invention Assignment Agreement, if applicable
5. Conflict of Interest Policy, if applicable
6. Absence and tardiness reporting
7. Probationary period
8. Wage assignments/garnishments
9. Use of time clock

Fig. 6-1   Checklist for orientation and induction program (sample 1).

GLOBE-UNION INC.

NEW EMPLOYEE CHECKLIST

The first two weeks are the most critical in determining whether the new employee will remain as an employee. To assist you in helping to develop a good start for all new employees the following checklist is provided. Each new employee will bring a checklist when he reports to you. Check all items as they are reviewed with the new employee. List the date (month and day) when this item was discussed. Forward completed checklist to the Employment Department within ten days of employee's start date. Both the new employee and you must sign the checklist copy. This copy will be filed in the employee's personnel folder in Employment.

FIRST DAY ON JOB

Foreman

_____ Hours of Work
_____ Promptness
_____ Lunch Hour
_____ Procedure to Leave Department
                and/or Plant
_____ Cleanup Time
_____ Attendance
_____ Shift Differential (if applies)
_____ Breaks
_____ Safety
_____ Smoking Restrictions
_____ Introduction to Fellow Workers

Leadman or Appointed Worker

_____ Time Clocks & Punching
_____ Emergency Exits
_____ First Aid Room
_____ Cafeteria Location
_____ Wash Room
_____ Tool Crib (if applies)
_____ Lockers or Cloakrooms
_____ Production Reports

WITHIN FIRST TEN WORKING DAYS

Foreman Responsibility

_____ Pay System—Incentive, Training Allowance, Boosts: Non-Incentive (whichever applies)
_____ Operator Training
_____ Probationary Period
_____ Job Changes
_____ Quality & Quantity
_____ Department Tour & Product Information

_____
Employee's Signature

_____
Employee's Clock Number

_____   _____
                Date   Foreman's Signature

Return completed checklist to Employment, Station H1

Fig. 6–2   Checklist for orientation and induction program (sample 2).

INDUCTION AND ORIENTATION CHECK LIST FOR SUPERVISORS

1. Find out and note background.
2. Relief and lunch.
3. Work safely (running, horseplay, housekeeping, hair, etc.)
4. Safety shoes and glasses.
5. Allen Bradley employee benefits—book issued.
6. Show gym and cafeteria—explain use—no gym relief—no cafeteria for afternoon relief.
7. Parking problem—their responsibility.
8. Show first aid—elsewhere out of bounds.
9. Clothing facilities—none at machine.
10. Rest rooms.
11. Introduction to set-up man and fellow workers.
12. Where to find supervisor or group leaders.
13. Two-week follow up to discuss performance.
14. Explain window problem.
15. Job sheets.
16. Overtime work—expect cooperation—department call in rule.
17. Starting and quitting time at the machine.
18. Show what we make.
19. Clothing (shorts, etc.)
20. Take on departmental tour.

Fig. 6-3   Checklist for orientation and induction program (sample 3).

In summary, the orientation of new employees is a critical area of responsibility for the foreman, the personnel department, and other key people. This is the time when new employees form opinions and attitudes about the company, the department, the foreman, and the work they will be assigned. It is the time when employee attitudes are created—either positive and enthusiastic or negative and unhealthy. If the orientation process is unpleasant, the new employee looks for employment elsewhere.

The orientation of employees is designed to furnish them with information and knowledge about the circumstances and conditions under which they will work. It should create positive attitudes and put the new employee in a proper frame of mind to learn the new job. It is the time when the new employee's anxieties, fears, and frustrations should be reduced and replaced with confidence, a feeling of belonging, and an enthusiastic attitude toward learning the new job. If the orientation program for new employees is done effectively, it will be easy to train a new employee to perform well.

TRAINING OF EMPLOYEES

The orientation of a new employee takes him up to the time when he will actually be trained and taught how to do a specific job. The stage should have been set so that the new employee is eager to learn and has no anxieties or fears about his ability to do the job. Also, the new employee should feel comfortable and at home in the department. He should have become acquainted with some of his fellow employees and of course should know his foreman.

The training process is very crucial, and it is in their training responsibility that many foremen, despite good intentions, fail. For this reason the balance of this chapter discusses the entire training process with special emphasis upon learning principles and training methods and techniques. We also consider the question of who should actually perform job training.

Principles of Learning

Before discussing the methods and techniques of training, it is important to consider the learner. We realize that it takes effort on the learner's part before learning can occur. This means that we must create a desire on the part of the learner to acquire the knowledge that we wish to impart. The principles of learning are no more than the means whereby this desire may be created.

Some specific principles of learning include:

1) *Readiness.* We have all seen a baseball game in which the pitcher sneaks a fast one over while the batter is still not quite ready. It is almost impossible to hit a baseball unless you are "all set." The same thing applies to training. Since the trainer is not trying to "sneak a fast one over," he must give the learner plenty of warning. He must get him ready—mentally as well as physically.

2) *Concentration.* Another principle important to efficient learning is concentration. We know some people learn rapidly while others learn more slowly. Some of this difference is in the learner's ability to concentrate, to focus all his attention on the task at hand. Some people have developed this trait to a very high degree; others find their attention constantly wandering. In the instruction process, the trainer must help the learner to concentrate by making the training interesting and by deliberately excluding as many distractions as possible.

3) *Repetition.* Another important principle is repetition. We learn by doing things over and over. That is the reason for practice on the football field or basketball floor. It is often necessary to repeat, repeat and repeat until every movement becomes second nature.

4) *Habit.* Habit is repetition applied to our actions. When we get up in the morning and dress, we do not have to think very carefully about what we are doing. This is true because of the habits we have long established. The trainer is concerned with helping the new man learn the proper habits. The sooner the new employee learns these habits, the sooner he will be free to turn his attention to the fine points of his job.

5) *Effect.* The so-called "Law of Effect" relates to the feeling of satisfaction we get when we have done something right. It might be pride of workmanship, it might be the satisfaction of hitting a golf ball 250 yards, it might be the praise of the teacher for work well done. When we get a positive response, we want to do it the same way again, so we'll get the same response.

Another way of looking at the learning process is to consider what makes learning difficult and what makes it easy. Factors that make learning difficult include:

1) Anxiety, nervousness, and fear of not being able to do the job, of having an accident, etc.
2) Conditions in which there is too much noise, dirt, or smoke, or other unsatisfactory physical conditions
3) Being under pressure to perform rapidly

4) Being unfamiliar with the terminology used by the instructor
5) Feeling that the job being learned is not important
6) Feeling that the person doing the instructing is not interested in the learner as an individual
7) Having an instructor who is impatient or very critical of early mistakes
8) Not being interested in learning the particular job.

The factors that make learning easy are also worth listing:

1) Being enthusiastic about learning the job
2) Feeling comfortable and at ease
3) Being in the right position to see and to hear what's going on
4) Being encouraged by the instructor
5) Having an instructor who is patient and willing to repeat things when necessary
6) Having the instructor use language that is readily understandable
7) Being trained in a physical climate that is conducive to learning—pleasant, relaxed, comfortable.

Who Should Do the Training?

After discussing learning principles, it seems obvious that there should be a number of characteristics required of an instructor who should be doing the training. One of the most difficult decisions is whether the foreman should personally do the training or whether another employee should do it. There is no one answer to this problem, but there are certain guidelines which will help an organization determine the answer for itself. The following characteristics of an effective teacher should be considered in choosing the individual who will do the training:

1) A positive attitude toward the department, toward his job, and toward the company
2) A desire to have the new employee learn the best way to do the job
3) A desire to teach
4) Effective communication skills—being able to get across an idea in terms that the other person can understand
5) Knowledge and skill of teaching principles and techniques
6) Patience
7) Willingness to prepare to teach
8) Time to teach
9) A warm friendly attitude toward the learner.

Typically, the foreman will have more of these characteristics than his employees, but not necessarily. One of the most critical of these is point 2 listed above. If, for example, an employee teacher has the other characteristics but doesn't really want this new employee to learn and to be effective as soon as possible, he is not the proper man to teach. Therefore, if the foreman is not personally going to do the teaching, he should take great care in selecting the employee to do it. Remember, the attitude, skill, and performance of the new employee depend to a large extent on the effectiveness of the instructor.

Training Methods and Techniques

The most frequently used method for teaching a person a new job is to actually perform the job right at the workplace. In other words, the trainer will bring a man into the department, show him where he's supposed to work, and proceed to teach him how to run the machine, assemble a product, or whatever else the job might be. Typically, this is done with other employees occupying adjacent workplaces engaged in work activities. In some companies, the new employee is under extreme pressure to learn because he is assigned initially to a production line and the effectiveness of the line depends on his own performance.

Some companies realize that such methods place undue pressure on the new employee and, therefore, are not the most effective way to teach him his job. Their approach is to remove the pressure of trying to learn while engaged in an actual production situation. There are several ways of doing this. One of them is simply to take the new worker into a separate part of the department where he can be taught under the right physical and mental conditions. A number of companies have set up what they call "vestibule training" in which they actually set up a separate training room that includes the same machines and situations existing on the job. Training specialists then teach people in this situation where they are not under pressure to produce; new workers do not get into the production line until they have been properly trained.

Regardless of physical training conditions, there are some very important principles to consider in training. These principles and steps were developed during the 1940s when a department of the government called "Training within Industry" developed a program called "Job Instruction Training (JIT)." These JIT principles and steps are still being widely used in industry today as a basis for training new employees. JIT is frequently called "the four-step method" because it consists of four basic steps:

Step 1—Prepare the Worker
    Put him at ease.
    State the job and find out what he already knows about it.
    Get him interested in learning his job.
    Place in correct position.
Step 2—Present the Operation
    Tell, show, and illustrate one important step at a time.
    Stress each key point.
    Instruct clearly, completely, and patiently, but no more than he can master.
Step 3—Tryout Performance
    Have him do the job—correct errors.
    Have him explain each key point to you as he does the job again.
    Make sure he understands.
    Continue until *YOU* know *HE* knows.
Step 4—Follow-Up
    Put him on his own. Designate to whom he goes for help.
    Check frequently. Encourage questions.
    Taper off extra coaching and close follow-up.

These four steps are widely accepted as being a practical approach for training anybody how to do almost any job. People who have not been trained in this four-step method frequently omit Step 1 and Step 3. In summary, Step 1 is designed to get the worker ready, physically and mentally, to learn the job. The general attitude of the instructor is very important. He must establish a good comfortable relationship or rapport with the new employee. He must remove the tensions and nervousness that are typical of a new employee. When Step 1 is properly done, the rest of the training can be much more effective.

Step 2 is designed to tell, show, and demonstrate the job that is to be done by the new employee. At this step the trainer's communication skills are extremely important because the employee must understand what the trainer is saying. Here is where empathy (putting yourself in the learner's shoes) is also important so that the trainer can readily tell if the employee understands the things that are being presented.

Step 3 is the one in which the employee actually tries to do the job *while the teacher is still there.* Many times in industry and business, a teacher who completes Step 2 leaves an employee on his own to sink or swim. It is essential that the teacher stay with the employee and watch to see how well he understands and how well he can do the job. If errors occur, they are corrected immediately by the instructor. The last point under Step 3 is most vital—"continue until you know he knows." In other words, the instructor should not leave the new employee until he is sure that the new employee can do the job on his own and will have a successful and pleasant experience in doing so.

Step 4 is the obvious follow-up to the training. Many foremen stay away too long before they return and check to see how the new employee is doing. It is recommended that the foreman stay away no longer than ten minutes. When he comes back to check on the employee, he has a very good opportunity to give him encouragement and praise if he is doing well. If he is making mistakes, it is the critical time to be there to correct these mistakes before they become habitual and before the employee becomes frustrated, discouraged, or embarrassed to the point of quitting.

All the way through these steps, it should be very obvious that the teacher should encourage the learner to ask questions.

The JIT slogan is, "If the worker hasn't learned, the instructor hasn't taught." This slogan contains an important piece of philosophy. It means that if the learner is making mistakes, the teacher should review himself and his own techniques to see where he may have failed. If the employee doesn't seem to understand, the instructor should examine his language and the approaches he has used in trying to teach the new employee. In other words, he should point the finger at himself for not having taught effectively rather than at the learner.

Preparing to Train

So far we have considered learning principles as well as teaching methods and techniques. The JIT approach includes some specific forms and procedures that should be used in preparing to train. These "makeready" steps include:

1) Have a time table; the time table should indicate the skill level you expect the learner to achieve and by what date.
2) Break down the job
   a. List important steps
   b. Pick out key points (safety is always a key point.)
3) Have everything ready, the right equipment, materials, and supplies.
4) Have the workplace properly arranged just as the worker will be expected to keep it.

Time Table. A suggested form has been developed for planning purposes. It is called the "Training Inventory and Time Table" and is intended to assist in answering two questions:

1) What skills do present employees have?
2) How much "depth" exists in the department—how many people can do each of the jobs?

The answers to these questions will help the foreman determine the training needs of his department. For example, how many people should be taught to do each of the jobs under his supervision in order to give him enough back-up men in case one or more of his workers is absent or quits? Also, these answers will tell him how many of the jobs should be taught to each employee to keep that employee challenged and happy.

Fig. 6-4 shows a form entitled "Training Inventory and Time Table." Specific jobs should be listed in the column headings at the top of the form. The names of present employees and each new employee should be listed on the left-hand side of the form. The steps for completing the form are:

1) Put an "x" in the appropriate boxes to indicate the jobs that each person can now perform.

Employee's Name	Haul Boards	Set Up Patterns	Mix Sand	Run the Sand Mullor	Pour Metal	Shake Down Castings		
T. Adams	X	–	–	–	–	–		
J. Brown	–	X	9/1/65	–	–	12/1/65		
D. Dowling	–	–	X	X	10/1/65	–		
H. Edsel	–	10/1/65	–	–	X	X		
J. Ford	X	X	X	X	9/1/65	X		
K. Cubics	X	9/1/65	X	12/1/65	3/1/66	X		
T. Kennedy	–	–	X	–	–	–		
R. Nichols	X	–	–	–	–	–		
P. Pigors	8/1/65	X	12/1/65	–	–	–		
S. Roberts	–	–	–	–	10/1/65	X		
T. Skzyz	8/1/65	–	X	–	–	–		
W. Thomas	8/1/65	9/1/65	10/1/65	X	12/1/65	3/1/66		

Legend: X means this worker can already do the job.
– means the worker does not need to know the job.
Date indicates when man will be trained to do the job.

Fig. 6–4 Training inventory and time table for employees supervised by the foreman in the molding department of a foundry.

JOB BREAKDOWN SHEET

JOB: Drilling hole

EQUIPMENT NEEDED: Drill press; jig; pieces

STEPS (*What* should be done)	KEY POINTS (*How* it should be done)
1. Fit piece in jig	Collar of piece in recess of jig
2. Tighten large thumb screw	
3. Tighten small thumb screw	
4. Start drill	With foot pedal
5. Oil drill	Use brush to apply small amount to tip of drill
6. Drill hole	a. Hold jig firmly b. Apply steady pressure on handle c. Ease up on handle when drill starts to cut through
7. Remove drill from piece	Raise handle to top
8. Remove part from jig	Loosen thumb screws
9. Stack piece in tote box	Hole to front end

Fig. 6–5 Job breakdown sheet for a drilling job.

2) Decide which jobs should be taught to each employee. Consider the needs of the department as well as the needs, desires, abilities, health, age, and interests of each person.

3) Where it is decided not to teach the job, insert a dash.

4) Where it is decided to teach an employee a job, insert the date for completing the training.

Break Down the Job. A form called a "Job Breakdown Sheet" has been developed so that the trainer can prepare to teach effectively. The form requires the trainer to list the job in a logical step-by-step basis. It shows the sequence of steps as well as key points for *how* to do the job. The "job breakdown sheet" becomes the step-by-step procedure to follow in presenting the operation to the employee. Fig. 6-5 shows a sample "job break-down sheet" for operating a drill press.

Have Everything Ready. This need, though obvious, is often ignored or forgotten. If things are not ready, it can reduce the effectiveness of the training by wasting time and by creating a negative attitude on the part of the learner.

Have Workplace Properly Arranged. Having the workplace properly arranged, with all tools, material, safety devices, etc., in their proper place has two advantages. First of all, it will assist the employee in learning the job, and second it provides him with an example of how the workplace should be kept in the future.

The Minority Worker

Much has been said and written concerning the orientation and training of minority workers, and indeed certain special factors should be considered. Overall, however, the same basic principles apply as in the orientation and training of other workers. Some of the characteristics of minority workers are described below, along with the implications for orientation and training procedures.

1) He may be intelligent, but barely able to read. Do not assume that he will read the pamphlets and items on the bulletin board.

2) He may have transportation problems so that any assistance from car pools, rides, bus information, or the like can be quite helpful in getting him to work on time.

3) His diet and eating habits may have been inadequate, so he may lack endurance and tire easily.

4) He is probably sensitive and easily discouraged. For example, being the only black in a white group may upset a man as much as it would to be the only white in a black group.

5) If new to industry, he is very "green" and needs good orientation and lengthy training.

6) Safety is a problem, due to inexperience, if he is new to industry.

7) Many times hostility is a mask for anxiety and tenseness. Making him feel welcome and at ease will help considerably.

8) He may be paying more for a less desirable place to live than the typical worker.

9) For the young, vocational advice and guidance is often quite lacking. He often has potential which he has never been encouraged to develop. In such cases, advice and training that assist him to grow in his work, or to secure a better job or higher rate, will probably not be acknowledged, but will assist in producing a loyal and valuable employee.

10) His attendance may not be as good as the typical worker because of his background, current family environment, health and transportation problems, etc.

The orientation and training of minority employees may be more difficult than for the typical worker. It requires an approach in which the personnel department and the foremen get this person properly oriented to the department, to the company, and to his job. The minority worker may come with a different background, attitudes, and aspirations which may not be applicable to the job. The job of orientation becomes important so that he does feel "at home" and also feels that somebody is taking a personal interest in him. His attitude toward the company, the job, and his boss are going to be important in terms of his future with the company. Therefore, the orientation procedure becomes very important and must be done effectively by both the personnel department and the foreman. Even within minority groups, a wide variation of attitudes, ambitions, experiences, and reasons for coming to work are present. Orientation, therefore, becomes a process that is tailored to the individual who is being hired.

The orientation and training of minority employees represents a major challenge. Sound approaches and techniques can and will work when properly applied by both staff personnel and line supervisors.

SUMMARY

The job of training is challenging and difficult. It is the responsibility of many people with the foreman being the key man. Obviously the foreman cannot do everything himself; he must have help, especially from the personnel and training departments. Members of these departments are specialists in both orientation and training. If they are knowledgeable in their field, they can provide tremendous help to the foreman and the foreman should rely upon them for any particular problems he might have. They should be qualified to formulate on-the-job techniques, to suggest such things as "vestibule training," or to develop specific techniques for training an employee on a specific job. If, for example, a foreman is faced with a job of training many people at one time, it becomes a group-training problem and the personnel or training department can help to solve it.

Also, there are probably other people in the company who can help the foreman fulfill his responsibility for employee orientation and training. These people might be in the industrial engineering department, in higher management, or at the foreman's own level. A foreman who does not feel qualified, or who for some other reason needs assistance, will probably look for help in his own department. Perhaps his group leader or one of his employees is an effective teacher and can do an effective job in training new employees. His qualifications and interests should be carefully considered.

In conclusion, the foreman is the key man in terms of the effective productivity of employees. A good program for orientation and training of new employees is essential to this effectiveness. Therefore, the foreman must take an active role. If he has not had the proper training and knowledge of effective indoctrination and instruction procedures, he should ask for help. A self-analysis of knowledge of training principles and approaches should be made. Selected items from the "Supervisory Inventory on Human Relations" (Fig. 6-6) are the kinds of questions that are relevant. He should learn the best principles and approaches by attending courses, by reading, and by learning from others. Likewise, he should set an example in training and improving himself. The example he sets in his own department will be absorbed by both new and experienced employees of the department and can have a real impact on the training that takes place under his supervision.

TRAINING

from
"Supervisory Inventory on Human Relations"
Dr. Donald L. Kirkpatrick
4380 Continental Drive
Brookfield, Wisconsin 53005

_____ 1. Most employees are interested in doing work of which they can be proud.

_____ 2. If a supervisor knows all about the work to be done, he is therefore qualified to teach others how to do it.

_____ 3. Teaching is complete only when the learner has learned.

_____ 4. Lack of interest accounts for more loafing on the part of employees than does laziness.

_____ 5. An employee's attitude has little effect on his production.

_____ 6. A supervisor cannot be expected to train his employees. He is too busy running his department.

_____ 7. When correcting the work an employee has been doing wrong, the supervisor should have the other employees observe so that they won't make the same mistake.

_____ 8. A well-trained working force is a result of maintaining a large training department.

_____ 9. In training an employee the first thing the supervisor should do is show in detail how the job is performed.

_____ 10. It's a bad policy for a supervisor to tell an employee, "I don't know the answer to your question, but I'll find out and let you know."

_____ 11. A supervisor would lose respect if he asked his employees for suggestions.

_____ 12. A good instruction rule is to emphasize how not to do the job.

_____ 13. The personnel or training department should be responsible to see that training is done in all departments.

_____ 14. An employee of average intelligence should be able to do a job after he is told and shown how it should be done.

_____ 15. A supervisor would be wasting his time talking with the employees about their families, interests, and outside-the-plant problems.

_____ 16. A knowledge of learning curves and plateaus is important to a supervisor.

_____ 17. The best way to train a new employee is to have him watch a good employee at the job.

_____ 18. Follow-up to see how an employee is doing isn't necessary if he got started in the right way.

_____ 19. Criticizing an employee for his mistakes will bring better results than praising him for his good work.

_____ 20. The training needs of a department should be determined by the supervisor in charge.

Fig. 6–6 Checklist on training. Check your knowledge of training by reading the list and recording your responses (true or false).
Answers: 1 2 3 4 5 6 7 8 9 10 11 12 13 14 15 16 17 18 19 20
          T, F T, T, F, F, F, F, F, F, F, F, T, F, F, T, F, F, F, T.

Chapter 7

The Foreman's Responsibility for Manufacturing Costs

Any enterprise, to stay in business, must produce high quality products, or at least produce products comparable to those offered by other firms in the same market. In addition, a company's products must be sold at a competitive price. If this competitive price is to be maintained, careful cost control is an absolute necessity.

To the foreman, the most meaningful depiction of day-by-day conditions is in terms of physical quantities—manpower, machine utilization, scrap, and material usage. These are important, but it is also necessary for the foreman to become familiar with his company's financial control system, the "dollarization" of his day-by-day operations. The foreman has a direct interest in cost control and in the financial control system since it is on the basis of costs that his department is judged. Without emphasis on costs a company's profit position would quickly deteriorate. The company would experience sales declines, and production cutbacks would be necessary. The foreman, at the front line of management, works at the point where the most significant cost savings would be made.

The foreman must be cost minded. This means that he must understand the need for cost control, must be continually on the outlook for situations where savings can be realized, and must be able to detect situations where costs are getting out of control. He should be knowledgeable concerning his costs, especially as related to direct labor, direct material, indirect labor, tooling, overhead, and supplies. Finally he must, in addition to being cost minded and knowing at all times what his costs are, be able to take effective cost control action.

Every member of management plays an important role in cost matters, but the first-line supervisor has one of the most important functions. The foreman has a direct interest in cost control since it reflects on his ability to manage his area as if "he were in business for himself." He furnishes data on a daily basis to show top management how actual performance, compared to plan, is progressing. He possesses the basic knowledge of how to make production at the right cost, and is the key to maintaining product quality while keeping unit costs competitive. He reports his problems to higher management, uses available resources, and takes the actions that are necessary to reduce unfavorable variances and improve the overall cost picture. When productivity drops, waste increases, and rising cost trends become evident, no one is better equipped to diagnose the problem and suggest corrective action than the first-line supervisor. He should be trained to be cost-minded, know where budgeted funds are being spent, and should be prepared to offer specific recommendations.

AREAS OF RESPONSIBILITY

The foreman's duties cover all operations as they apply on the floor or in the office, and he is held responsible for the day-to-day activities in terms of: (1) number of parts produced, (2) number of scrapped pieces, (3) number of man hours used (direct and indirect), (4) machine utilization, and (5) material used.

The foreman has direct control over some of these items, while for others he has to be assisted by the responsible service departments, for example, by the quality control department and maintenance department. The foreman's basic responsibilities, those of prime importance, are listed below. It is these areas that require his attention and problem-solving knowledge.

1) Direct labor
2) Direct material
3) Indirect support labor
4) Indirect materials
   a. Tooling
   b. Supplies
   c. Other manufacturing expenses
5) Scrap and rework
6) Safety
7) Housekeeping
8) Human relations.

Direct Labor

Direct costs are those that may be traced directly to a unit of production. *Direct labor* is that labor which changes the physical shape of a product and can be accurately allocated by a foreman to a specific part, operation, or process.

An example from the automobile industry will help to illustrate the direct labor concept. A car door is stamped in the press department, gas-welded in the welding department, and painted with a primer coat in the finishing department. The direct labor cost is the cost of wages, fringe benefits, etc., incurred for the employees who operate the press, welding, and painting equipment. The door is more valuable after the painting operation than it was before being stamped out in the pressworking department. This increase in value is due in large part to the direct labor used in making the door.

Direct Material

Direct material is the material that becomes part of the finished item, subassembly, or product. Direct material includes both raw stock such as cold-rolled steel or iron ingots and standard finished items such as screws, clamps, and nuts and bolts. The foreman is responsible for seeing that direct material used in the product conforms to engineering specifications, and that the material is of the proper quality. Failure to check on material can result in machine downtime and can lead to unfavorable direct labor cost variances while machines are stopped. If poor material is not detected until after products are manufactured, scrap and reject rates can rise to unacceptable and costly levels.

Indirect Labor

Indirect labor is just as necessary as direct labor, but does not involve the fabrication or assembly of the product or its components. Indirect labor includes the wages and other costs of supervisory personnel, material handlers, clerical personnel, maintenance employees, and setup men. Supervisory personnel include the foreman himself as well as general foremen, department managers, and superintendents.

The foreman must supervise indirect labor closely because it is often nonrepetitive in nature and is more difficult to assign and control. Indirect labor requirements are generally determined on the basis of direct labor work content hours required in a productive department for a pre-established volume of production.

The quantity and skill of indirect labor to support direct labor hours at different productive levels are established by the industrial engineering department in conjunction with the affected first-line supervisor and the controller's office.

Fig. 7-1 illustrates a sample manning table reflecting the direct and indirect labor requirements for a machine shop department. For the different direct labor volume requirements the indirect support labor by function is shown. The nonvariable manpower indicates the indirect labor requirements by function that will not vary with production output and will have to be maintained at lower rates of production.

MANNING TABLE
PLANT B – MACHINING DEPARTMENT

Functional Description	Control Volume	80%	90%	100%	110%	120%	130%
	Base Labor	36	29	32	35	38	42
	Non-Variable Manpower	Manpower	Manpower	Manpower	Manpower	Manpower	Manpower
Salary							
Foreman-Machining	2	3	3	3	3	3	4
Supervisor-Inspection	1	1	1	1	1	1	1
Clerk	1	1	2	2	2	2	3
Total Salary	4	5	6	6	6	6	8
Hourly							
Jobsetter	–	4	4	5	5	5	6
Tool Grinder	1	3	3	3	3	4	4
Crib Attendant	1	1	1	1	1	1	1
Material Handler	1	4	5	5	6	6	6
Inspector	–	4	5	5	5	6	6
Clean-Up	1	2	2	2	2	2	3
Crane Operator	1	1	1	1	1	1	1
Fork Truck Driver	1	1	1	1	1	1	1
Total Hourly	6	20	22	23	24	26	28
Total Department	10	25	28	29	30	32	36

Fig. 7-1 Manning table for a machinery department.

Indirect Material

Indirect materials are materials used in the manufacturing process which do not become a part of the final product. Two important categories of indirect materials are tooling and supplies.

Tooling. Foremen are responsible for seeing that tools are cleaned, sharpened, and adjusted regularly. Failure to observe proper tooling maintenance and control procedures will result in lowered production rates and higher scrap and reject rates. In the narrowest sense tooling considerations are associated with production machinery such as lathes, milling machines, grinders, and broaches, but other production equipment (sewing machines, welding equipment, etc.) must also be maintained to assure the best results. All the machinery and equipment used in fabrication, assembly, and test operations should be kept in top shape to assure lowest cost operations. The foreman should observe the machinery and equipment in his department carefully, and should call to the service department's attention day-to-day malfunctions in any of the tooling.

Supplies. The foreman is also responsible for the nonproduction materials essential to the production process. These supplies are used under the supervision of the foreman and should be controlled by him. Failure to watch over supplies can result in wastage or stockouts. Supplies can include items such as abrasives, brooms and brushes, solder, rags, paper towels, acetylene oxygen, and pencils and stationery.

Other Indirect Costs. There are certain other indirect costs that the foreman may not control but of which he should be aware. Such items as power, heat, air, lighting, telephone service, building rent, and taxes are good examples. Normally costs such as these are lumped together in one account and charged to individual departments as overhead or factory burden.

One other group of costs is worth mentioning at this point—the indirect costs associated with employees. In most factories a pre-established labor rate is charged for each hour worked by employees within certain classifications. In other words, instead of charging just the employee's hourly wage rate, a rate is used that includes fringe benefits—hospitalization insurance, cost of living allowance, holiday pay, welfare fund, pensions, severance pay, etc. The foreman should be aware of how these kinds of costs are charged to his department, but more important he should use his employees efficiently to assure that these expenses are not excessive. Employees not needed on a particular day, for example, can be reported to the central office for temporary reassignment. The union contract may limit the foreman's discretion in such matters, but the foreman is responsible for using his employees as efficiently as possible subject to any such restrictions.

Scrap and Rework

The foreman has a direct interest in quality control since he is evaluated partly on the basis of his performance in this area. Producing two parts in order to have one good part is no way to run a department. The defective part will either have to be scrapped or reworked. Scrapping parts results in unfavorable direct material variances from budgeted amounts, and reworking operations raise the cost of labor.

The foreman must strive for quality workmanship, however. If the operator produces defective items, it is necessary that the foreman first check all the possible conditions associated with the job, i.e., the process, mechanical failures, materials, etc., before assuming it is the fault of the operator. It is the foreman's responsibility to select the proper employee to perform the work, to instruct the operator how to use the machine, and to furnish the correct tools and materials.

The quality control department can assist the foreman, but QC has no magic formula to insure product quality. Good quality must be built into the product as the product is being manufactured. The primary responsibility rests with the production foreman, who is responsible for:

1) Producing parts, subassemblies, or assemblies in accordance with engineering specifications so that they meet the prescribed quality standards.
2) Working in close harmony with all plant services to assure proper functioning of equipment, tools, gages, machines, mechanical handling devices, and processes in order that quality work will be performed.
3) Being alert to quality problems which arise because of another department's activities, and cooperating with other departments to correct such problems.
4) Taking such action as is necessary, through organizational channels and by prescribed procedures, to obtain immediate correction of quality defects.

There are certain internal and external programs provided to assist the foreman in identifying and reducing scrap and rework. These include Zero Defects, Value Analysis, and Preventive Maintenance.

Zero Defects. Zero Defects is a motivational program aimed at inspiring the individual to strive toward producing defect-free work. It puts the responsibility for quality performance squarely on the shoulders of the individual, making each man his own critic, and re-emphasizes pride in workmanship.

Zero defects is based on the principle of prevention rather than detection of errors. It stresses the importance of good workmanship in which the individual can take pride and receive recognition. This program recognizes that employees want to do good work, and can achieve a high degree of perfection in what they do if properly motivated.

The objectives of a Zero Defects program are:

1) To motivate the individual to do the job right the first time, to prevent defects caused by human error
2) To provide individual and/or group recognition for good workmanship
3) To develop a spirit of teamwork as well as competition among individuals or groups to promote good work
4) To inform the individual of the importance of the work he does to the overall success of the firm
5) To develop the realization that personal security is related to the accomplishment of quality workmanship
6) To reduce the cost of error correction
7) To improve product quality
8) To remove the causes of error.

Shown in Fig. 7-2 is a form used in identifying errors. Each employee is encouraged to become aware of the aspects of his own job which might result in errors, and he is urged to report any areas that need correction. An alternative form is shown as Fig. 7-3

To be effective the Zero Defects must be properly integrated into the mainstream of line management. It must have top management's support and should be a regular part

ERROR CAUSE IDENTIFICATION

The following cause of error should be investigated in working toward the goal of Error Free Performance.

Errors are caused on my job because:

Submitted By:

Name _____   Date _____

Department _____   Supervisor _____

Fig. 7–2   Form used to report potential causes of job errors.

of each supervisor's daily routine. Zero Defects is a personal appeal to each employee to dedicate himself. Because it is a personal appeal, it must be made by the employee's immediate supervisor. The first-line supervisor will make the program a success.

Value Analysis. Value analysis is an analytical type of program designed to examine all the components of cost of an existing or new product in order to determine

ZERO DEFECTS

ERROR CAUSE IDENTIFICATION

NAME		LOCATION	MAIL POINT
OCCUPATION TITLE	DEPT.	CLOCK NO.	☐ HOURLY ☐ SALARY

IN ORDER THAT A BETTER JOB BE PERFORMED TOWARD THE GOAL OF ERROR FREE PERFORMANCE, I AM IDENTIFYING THE FOLLOWING CAUSE OR POTENTIAL CAUSE OF ERROR:

SUPERVISOR'S COMMENTS

SUPERVISOR'S NAME	ROUTE FOR ACTION TO: (NAME)	DATE TO BE RETURNED

Fig. 7–3   Alternative form for use in reporting potential causes of job errors.

whether or not any item of cost can be reduced or eliminated while retaining all functional and quality requirements.

Value analysis is an organized, creative approach to the identification and elimination of unnecessary costs while maintaining consistently high quality. It is a team effort with a formal plan and has members from the different company activities. It is a dynamic activity which thrives on well-considered change without compromising quality. Many times these teams have found that a simple change in design or method will improve quality and reduce scrap and rework at the same time.

For example, value analysis may lead to:

1) Use of different materials
2) A new design requiring fewer parts
3) A cheaper or less expensive manufacturing method
4) Improved quality through simplified or improved assembly techniques.

The foreman receives the benefit of the value analysis effort to reduce waste, improve quality, and lower production costs. He plays an important role in identifying design, material, and operating inefficiencies needing correction. The value analysis team should include a representative from the manufacturing area so that the production viewpoint can be expressed, and the foreman should know who this representative is so that he may convey any suggestions or viewpoints he may have to the committee.

When the foreman detects an area that he thinks can be improved through value analysis, he can refine his ideas by examining them according to the outline presented below:

Function
　1) Are all the functions essential to the working of the assembly?
　2) What other ways are there of achieving the same function?
　3) Can any or all of the functions performed by this component be incorporated into another component?

Material Specification
　1) Can any other specification of the same type of material be used?
　2) Can any other material be used?

Material Waste
　1) Can the waste be reduced by a minor design modification?
　2) Can the waste be reduced by changing the method of manufacture?

Process of Manufacture
　1) Can the finished component be produced by a different method of manufacture?
　2) Can the component be made more easily in more than one piece?
　3) Can a different process of manufacture be used which will reduce or eliminate any labor operations?

Standardization
　1) Can the manufactured component be replaced by a standard part?
　2) Can the raw material be standardized to advantage?

Direct Labor Costs
　1) Can any labor operation be eliminated or reduced by a minor design change, by a change in method of manufacture, or by improved machinery and equipment?
　2) Can any assembly operations be reduced?

Direct Material Costs

1) Can the costs of packing, handling, or transportation be reduced?
2) Do the ordering quantities and methods achieve optimum benefits for the company?
3) Can an alternative reliable supplier be found to furnish raw materials or partially finished parts at lower cost?

Besides value analysis there are other cost reduction programs used in manufacturing. They are called by various names, for example, methods improvement, work simplification, methods engineering, profit improvement, and value engineering.

The most important common feature of all of these programs is that each of them, like value analysis, permits all departments to participate in cost control efforts. Cost reduction involves more than just cutting out obvious instances of waste. It is a matter of making every expenditure produce the greatest possible value. What is often needed is a better way of doing something, and the foreman has an important role, no matter what the program is called, in seeking out and offering systematic approaches for reducing operating costs.

Preventive Maintenance. The maintenance function exerts a definite influence on production costs, either because of its labor cost or through its effect on production downtime and unit quality. The efficiency with which direct labor is used is directly related to machinery and equipment downtime. It is obvious that employees cannot be sent home every time a piece of production equipment fails to operate properly, and the wages of idle employees must continue to be paid even though nothing is being produced. The result is an unfavorable direct labor cost variance and a higher labor cost per unit of production.

The prevention of downtime is everyone's responsibility. Machine operators should be instructed to inform their foreman of any difficulties. If maintenance services are needed, the foreman should call the maintenance department. Fig. 7-4 provides an example of a Maintenance Request Form that may be used for this purpose.

When major repairs are necessary the foreman in conjunction with the production control department may decide upon advanced production runs to build up a bank and thus free the machine for repair. The foreman, maintenance department, and production control department must work closely together to achieve proper coordination.

The foreman should carefully observe the machinery and equipment in his area. He must maintain records of equipment downtime, be aware of cyclic inspection requirements and preventive measures such as the cleaning and disassembling of fixtures, conveyors, and chains. He must be aware of lubrication schedules and he has to provide feedback to the maintenance department regarding causitive factors for equipment malfunctions so that appropriate action can be planned. A carefully scheduled preventive maintenance program should be developed to minimize breakdowns and loss of production. Machine interruptions, as mentioned earlier, cause direct labor losses, and labor costs begin pyramiding when premium overtime is required to make up lost production. Prolonged interruptions not only cause production losses, but quality may also decline. Preventive maintenance is nothing more than planned maintenance, taking care of minor problems and servicing requirements before emergencies develop.

The foreman should make daily visual inspections of the machinery and equipment in his area, seek out problems from the operators, and forward this information to the maintenance department. This approach can virtually eliminate major equipment fail-

```
┌──────────────────────────────────────────────────────────────────────┐
│                      REQUEST FOR MAINTENANCE                           │
│                                                                        │
│  TO _____                                   │
│                                                                        │
│  FROM _____      DATE _____    │
│                                                                        │
│  _____    _____    _____          │
│   EQUIPMENT NAME       BRASS TAG NUMBER        LOCATION                 │
│                                                                        │
│  _____    _____    _____          │
│   TIME REQUIRED        DATE AVAILABLE          DATE REQUIRED            │
│                                                                        │
│  _____    _____    _____          │
│     PART NAME            PART NUMBER        BANK REQD. (IN DAYS)        │
│  REMARKS _____ │
│                                                                        │
│  _____  │
│                          Requesting Activity:                          │
│  _____  │
│                                                                        │
│  Info Copy to:                                                         │
│  Maintenance Dept.    Prod. Control   Manufacturing   Tool Stores   Industrial Engrg. │
│                                                                        │
└──────────────────────────────────────────────────────────────────────┘
```

Fig. 7-4   Typical form used by foremen to request maintenance services.

ures. By anticipating equipment problems, the foreman can detect many of them before the problems become serious.

Vendors. By working closely with vendors the foreman can often reduce the costs associated with scrap and rework. By checking on the quality of incoming materials, for example, the foreman can detect bad material before it reaches his machines. Actually, the foreman may not always perform such an inspection himself since this is normally the function of the quality control department, but he should be conscious of potential problems in this area. He should screen any vendor-supplied parts or materials coming into his department, and he should report on a regular basis any rework problems that these materials or parts may be causing. By making such reports the foreman gives the quality control department the information it needs to work with vendors in maintaining high quality standards.

Machine and Equipment Manufacturers. Prompt reports from the foreman regarding machinery and equipment, especially new installations, are valuable to higher management in working with machine and equipment manufacturers. New machinery installed in a department is often covered by service and performance warranties. Timely and detailed reports are necessary in order to determine whether new installations are performing according to expectations.

In many instances companies send their foremen to the machine builder's plant to learn about the machinery before the new installation is made in the factory. This procedure is a good one, and often results in the elimination of potential problems before the actual factory installation is made. Regardless of the specific program followed by a company, higher management should realize that the foreman, by virtue of his knowledge and experience, is in a good position to provide information useful in dealing with machine and equipment suppliers. Failure to use the foreman in this way can result in excessive costs and loss of production because of downtime.

Safety Practices

Bad safety practices can result in tragic accidents as well as higher costs. The foreman is probably the most important person in the plant in maintaining a good safety program and keeping the accident rate down.

The foreman must continually practice and preach safety. He should respond promptly and report unsafe conditions to the proper authority. Safety should be a major part of the foreman's job and, in turn, of the jobs of his employees.

Costs incurred in accidents include both direct and indirect costs:

Direct Costs
    Medical treatment
    Damaged equipment
    Workmen's compensation claims
Indirect Costs
    Wages of injured employees
    Inefficiency of injured employees
    Disruption of workforce

The foreman should instruct every new employee in safety practices and policies, and he should regularly remind all department members of the established safety rules. Infractions of safety rules should be watched for, and employees violating established rules should be warned, and the infractions stopped. It is also a good idea for the foreman to seek ideas from his employees regarding safety practices, and to either act upon these suggestions or if that is not possible report them to higher management.

While it is not our purpose to dwell upon safety, a few of the major causes of accidents are worth mentioning:

1) Failing to use guards provided or operating unguarded machine
2) Failing to adjust guards properly, or not replacing guards after removal during maintenance
3) Trying to clean or oil a machine while it is in motion
4) Trying to clear obstructions without shutting off the power
5) Failing to lock out the power switch when performing maintenance work
6) Doing work not designed for the machine
7) Overloading machine, causing machine failure
8) Failing to perform proper maintenance resulting in machine failure
9) Dressing improperly
10) Makeshift repairs
11) Horseplay

Housekeeping

The foreman should strive to keep his work area neat and tidy. Sloppy, dirty workplaces breed inefficiency and laxness. It is difficult to maintain a cost-conscious, safety-minded attitude on the part of workers in such an environment. Ample trash cans should be provided; a clean eating area should be set aside for lunch and coffee breaks; a clean drinking fountain is needed; and racks or lockers should be furnished for the storage of clothing and other personal belongings. Metal chips should be cleaned regularly from machining areas, and cleaning rags and other flammable materials should be stored carefully. Operators should be made responsible for the appearance of their own work areas, and it is desirable to set aside a few minutes at the end of the day as clean-up time.

Human Relations

We will not discuss the foreman's human relations responsibilities in detail since this was the topic of Chapter 5. It is worth noting again, however, that high morale is a factor in achieving an effective, efficient department. Happy employees tend to work harder, and a pleasant, enjoyable working environment also tends to reduce the costs associated with absenteeism. A contented workforce is also likely to achieve higher quality production, and scrap and rework costs should decline accordingly.

THE COST REPORTING SYSTEM

Proper control of costs requires an extensive cost reporting system. To function effectively the foreman needs to understand how this system works and what role he plays in the system.

Fig. 7-5 shows a flow chart indicating how the direct labor performance report is compiled in a typical company. The foreman (see first column) is responsible for using the required amount of direct labor to achieve production objectives. He prepares a daily record of the number of hours worked by each employee in his department. Normally he prepares this report at the end of his shift.

The foreman's report goes to the timekeeping department in the controller's office (see second column). Here the timekeeper checks the foreman's report against the time

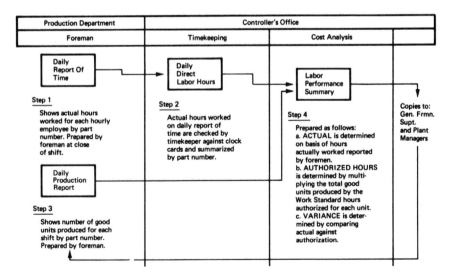

Fig. 7-5   Flow chart showing how direct labor performance report is compiled.

clock cards and summarizes the total number of hours worked according to part number, job number, or some similar criteria. Along with the timekeeping department's labor hour summary, the foreman's production report (Step 3 in Fig. 7-5) goes to the cost analysis section of the controller's office. Here a labor performance summary report is prepared for higher management.

As the cost reporting flow indicates, the foreman is the "finger tips" of management. He is responsible for using the resources of the company and for reporting the results for measurement against pre-established standards. If he fails in either of these tasks he has failed in his basic cost responsibility.

Feedback

Feedback is an integral part of the cost reporting system. When the foreman reports the current week's, day's or shift's performance, this performance data is analyzed by the controller's office, compared to pre-established standards, and variances from standard, either favorable or unfavorable, are then in turn reported back to the foreman.

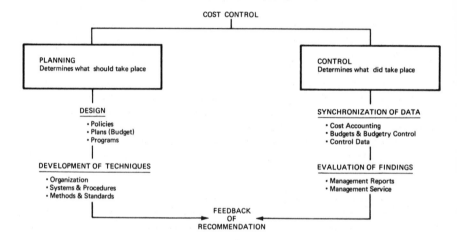

Fig. 7-6   Schematic representation of the cost control reporting and feedack system.

This reverse reporting, or feedback, allows the foreman to compare his actual performance to the ideal or standard that was expected of him. It also allows him to determine in which cost areas his department is weak and in which ones it is strong. By concentrating on the weak areas he can attempt to improve departmental performance during the next reporting period. Without timely and complete feedback the foreman would be working in the dark; he would not know his weaknesses and would not know what areas to concentrate on to achieve improvements.

Fig. 7-6 shows a schematic representation of the cost control reporting and feedback system. Notice particularly the role of planning and control in this system.

Reports

A wide variety of reports are required to keep track of essential manufacturing costs. Regardless of the type of report, the information it contains must be up to date. Examples of several types of reports are shown in Figs. 7-7, 7-8, 7-9, and 7-10.

DAILY DIRECT LABOR PERFORMANCE

PLANT A B C   DATE_____

DEPARTMENT	FOREMEN	SHIFT	HOURS			% EFF.	MANHOURS		MANPOWER	
			AUTH	ACTUAL	% OFF STD.		SAVINGS	EXCESS	SAVINGS	EXCESS
SUPT: N. Jones										
71	J. SMITH	1	1676.2	2120.1	26.5	79.1		443.9		55.5
	G. BROWN	2	1106.8	1272.1	14.9	87.0		105.3		20.7
	W. GREER	3	571.3	848.0	48.4	67.3		276.7		34.6
	TOTAL		3354.3	4240.2	26.4	79.1		885.9		110.8
SUPT: A. Ward										
72	T. BLACK	1								
	F. WHITE	2								
	G. GRAY	3								
	TOTAL									
SUPT: C. Bills										

DAILY DIRECT LABOR PERFORMANCE

PLANT _____   VARIANCE LETTER   DATE _____

SUPT: N. Jones

DEPT. 71

EXPLANATION OF VARIANCE

	OFF-STANDARD	
	MANHOURS	MANPOWER
DIE TROUBLE AND DIE REPAIR— MACHINES B.T. NOS 3731-3693 PERFORMING PRIMARY OPERATIONS ON PART NO. 359694 · REAR DECK FLOOR SIDE PAN RT	50.4	6.3
CHANGING PERSONNEL AROUND FOR "HOT JOBS" AND "MUST RUN" JOBS.	24.0	3.0

Fig. 7-7   Direct labor performance report and accompanying variance letter.

    With each of these performance reports is included a variance letter. The purpose of the variance letter is to explain any unfavorable variance included in the report. Note for example the variance letter accompanying the direct labor performance report shown in Fig. 7-7.

    The daily reports submitted by the foreman are frequently combined into weekly reports by the controllers office in order to give higher management a condensed view of manufacturing cost performance. The controller's office may also chart the results of the foreman's daily reports over some longer period of time in order to develop trends.

    The obvious reason for these reports is to provide higher management with objective criteria for evaluating performance. In addition, however, management, by studying trends that develop, can detect costs that are going out of control and assist the foreman in taking appropriate corrective action.

    As mentioned, all of the reports shown include a variance letter. All variances or departures from budgeted amounts must be identified and explained. By being aware of the reasons for unfavorable variances, the plant manager can evaluate the facts and provide the necessary assistance to eliminate them. If a variance occurs frequently, this may indicate that the standard cost has been set too low and should be revised upward. In

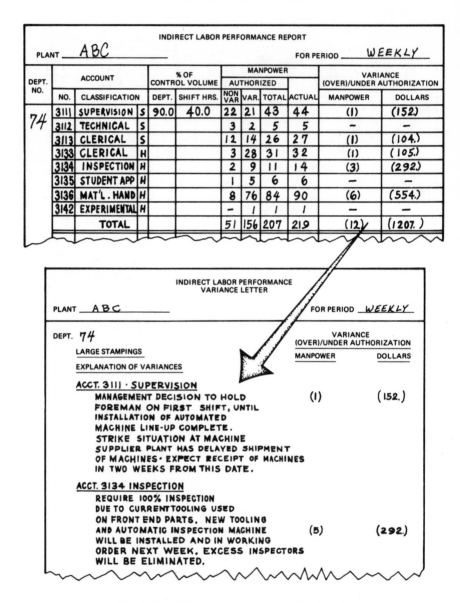

Fig. 7–8   Indirect labor performance report and variance letter.

MANUFACTURING BUDGET PERFORMANCE REPORT

OTHER MANUFACTURING EXPENSE

D. L. $15,553.
PERIOD _MONTH OF MAY_

PLANT __A BC__
DEPT. __94X__

NO.	NAME	VAR. RATE	FIXED AND NON-VAR.	VARIABLE	TOTAL	ACTUAL	DOLLARS	%	BUDGET	VARIANCE	%
	ACCOUNT		BUDGET AUTHORIZATION				VARIANCE		YEAR-TO-DATE		
3631	FUEL – POW.&PRO.	7.62	1171.	1185.	2356	2421	(65)	(2.8)	7500.	(160)	(2.1)
3632	FUEL - PUR.OUT.	.47	12.	73.	85	82	3	3.5	255.	(17)	(6.7)
	SUB-TOTAL FUEL	8.09	1183.	1258	2441	2503	(62)	(2.5)	7755.	(177)	(2.3)
	ALL OTHER	11.48	319.	1785	2104	2375	(271)	(12.9)	647l.	(388)	(6.0)
3600	TOTAL SUPPLIES	19.57	1501.	3043	4545	4878	(333)	(7.3)	14226.	(565)	(4.0)
3716	TAXES– REAL PROP.	–	843		843	843	–	–	2529	–	–
3712	" MACH.&EGR	–	1005		1005	1120	(115)	11.4	3015	(115)	(38)
3716	" INVENTORY	–	1192		1192	1294	(102)	(8.6)	3576.	(93)	(26)
3720	DEP.– BUILDINGS	–	904		904	904	–	–	2712	–	–
3700	TOTAL FIXED EXP.	–	3944		3944		(227)	(58)	11832	(208)	–

MANUFACTURING BUDGET PERFORMANCE

OTHER MANUFACTURING EXPENSE

VARIANCE LETTER

PLANT __ABC__   FOR PERIOD _____   DEPT. __94X__

EXPLANATION OF VARIANCES	VARIANCE (OVER)/UNDER AUTHORIZATION
3600 ACCT. SERIES – SUPPLIES	($333.00)
UNNOTICED UNDERGROUND PIPE LINE LEAK ACCOUNTED FOR 150 GAL. LOSS OF DIESEL OIL.	
REPLENTISH DIESEL OIL SUPPLY	(65.00) (65.00)
CHANGE OVER TO M-164 LUBRICANT AS AUTHORIZED BY MASTER MECHANIC. PURCHASED 10 DRUMS @ 25.00 PER DRUM	(250.00)
10 DRUMS OF M-162 FORMERLY USED BEING RETURNED TO SUPPLIER FOR CREDIT–NEXT WEEK – VALUE $240.00	
EXCESS GLOVE USAGE	(15.00)
PRICE INCREASE — OXYGEN AND ACETYLENE — NOT ANTICIPATED.	(6.00) (271.00)
	(336.00)
MISCELLANEOUS	3.00
	(333.00)

Fig. 7–9   Other manufacturing expense performance report and variance letter.

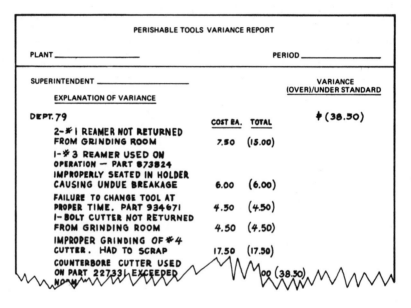

Fig. 7–10 Perishable tool performance report and variance letter.

order for the standard cost system to function properly it is absolutely essential for the foreman to report his variances and provide the best explanation for them that he can.

Accurate reports are a necessity. Top management acts upon reports based on information furnished by the foreman, and if top management's actions are based on inadequate information it is obvious that these actions will likewise be inadequate. The foreman must train himself to be honest in reporting current performance. Unfortunately, some foremen have experienced situations in which they have been made to feel that unfavorable variances are a reflection on their personal efficiency. Of course, this is not always the case. Unfavorable variances can be created by many factors—poor quality material, a bad process, new and untrained employees, etc. In other cases the budgeted figures themselves may be wrong. This frequently happens when standard costs are established without the participation of the foreman.

The foreman's best course of action is to report the operating facts exactly as they occur in his department. If unfavorable variances result, he should always explain the cause for them. If he feels that the standard cost is too low or high, then he should request that it be raised or lowered and explain his reasoning. The effective operation of a standard cost system requires cooperation and candor among the foreman, the accounting department, and higher management. The true purpose of a well-designed, properly functioning cost control system is the improvement of operating efficiency, not the harassment of operating personnel.

Reported Items

Reports from the foreman usually cover labor utilization, scrap and rework, overtime, and equipment utilization. Each of these are discussed below.

Labor Utilization. One of the most significant inputs to the cost control system is the labor utilization report. Labor production is measured in terms of the number of good parts produced by the department during a particular shift. Fig. 7-11 shows a daily production report used in one company for the foremen to report output figures for each days shift. This report goes to the budget office, timekeepers office, controller's office, or other office designated within the company to compile the labor utilization report. The daily production report indicates net production—gross production less scrap and rework. The *net production* figure is multiplied by the standard time per unit, and the extension of this operation is listed as *authorized standard hours*. The formula used is:

Net Production × Unit Standard Hours = Authorized Standard Hours

The timekeeping department then determines the total number of hours actually worked from an examination of employee time cards. The authorized standard hours divided by the actual hours worked gives the labor utilization, as follows:

Labor Utilization (%) = (Authorized Standard Hours/Actual Hours) × 100

DAILY PRODUCTION REPORT				
Dept. No.	Date		Foreman	
40	Dec. 29, 1971		Steve Owen	
Part No.	SHIFT			
	1	2	3	Total
230	740			740
234	1300			1300
261	1600			1600
266	400			400
274	1600			1600
278	1120			1120
283	1241			1241
293	2200			2200
301	–			–
327	–			–

Fig. 7-11   Daily production report used by foreman to report output.

For example, when the authorized standard hours equals 10, and the actual hours equals 8, then:

$$\text{Labor Utilization} = (10/8) \times 100$$
$$= 125\%$$

When the authorized standard hours equals 6, and the actual hours equals 8, then:

$$\text{Labor Utilization} = (6/8) \times 100$$
$$= 75\%$$

Obviously, labor utilization below 100 percent is unfavorable.

The main purpose of the labor utilization report is to assist the foreman in monitoring and improving the use of direct labor. The foreman who simply reports his daily production figures and files away the standard cost report that he receives back from the accounting department is overlooking an important management tool that is available to him.

In many companies the foreman is forced to make use of this management tool by being required to prepare and forward a daily analysis report. An example, based on the daily production report of Fig. 7-11, is shown in Table VII-1. Note that each employee is listed by badge number in the first column. The report then shows which part the employee worked on, the number that employee produced, the standard unit hour allowance for that particular part, and the total number of standard hours allowable. The next two columns list the actual hours worked and the excess hours over the standard allowable amount. In the last column the foreman provides an explanation for unfavorable variances. If the variance were favorable an explanation would also be desirable since management would be interested in knowing how the improvement was achieved. The reasons given in this report for unfavorable variances are typical reasons; note that in several instances these variances are not the fault of anyone in particular but rather represent unavoidable machine malfunctions.

This report allows the foreman to pinpoint his problems and arrive at solutions. Unfavorable variances because of operator inefficiency suggest the need for operator training. Excessive variances caused by machine and equipment downtime may mean that maintenance needs to be improved. Variances caused by bad materials may mean that incoming quality control needs improvement.

In a company where foremen are not asked to prepare daily analysis reports, it is suggested that the foreman himself should consider keeping a record such as this for his own use. If you think back to remember the kinds of questions that you may have been asked about departmental performance, you can easily imagine the advantage you would have in replying to such questions if such records were available to you.

Scrap and Rework Report. The foreman's labor utilization report is based on the number of *good* parts produced. Before reporting his net production figure (using the form shown in Fig. 7-11) he must receive a scrap and rework report from the quality control department (see Fig. 7-12). This report tells him how many of the parts leaving his department as finished work were unacceptable and had to be rejected. These parts are then subtracted from the foreman's gross production figure to arrive at a net production figure.

Table VII-1. Foreman's Daily Analysis Report.

Dept. # 40   Group 4   Date: December 29th   Foreman: Steve Owen

Badge No.	Working on Part	Pieces Produced	Unit Std. Hr. Allow.	Total Std. Hrs.	Actual Hrs.	Excess Hrs.	Reason for Off-Standard
16	230	740	.0090	6.7	8.0	1.3	Machine not anchored properly. Speed and feed reduced to hold tolerance.
13	234	500	.0100	5.0	8.0	3.0	Staggered machine breakdown. Temporary repairs made. Machine repair part not in stock—obsolete.
13	261	1600	.0040	6.4	8.0	1.6	Operator inefficiency
17	266	400	.0200	8.0	8.0	—	None
14	274	1600	.0037	5.9	8.0	2.1	Scaled steel clogged collet on screw machine #444 causing excess scrap parts and machine downtime to clean.
19	278	1120	.0060	6.7	8.0	1.3	Automatic chip drag not functioning properly. Had to shut down machine periodically to remove chips.
18	283	1241	.0062	7.7	8.0	.3	Operator inefficiency
15	293	2200	.0031	6.8	8.0	1.2	Operator not positioning blank properly causing crimp—resulting in scrap.
11	234	800	.0100	8.0	8.0	—	None
				61.2	72.0	10.8	

Referring back to Fig. 7-12, note that it was necessary to scrap 115 units of part number 230, and 300 units of part number 274. The foreman's daily analysis report in Table VII-1 shows that unfavorable variances occur with respect to both of these parts. The foreman's explanation for the variances indicates that machine and material problems contributed to the scrap problem.

SCRAP REPORT				
DEPT. *40* GROUP *4*	DATE *12-29*	FOREMAN *STEVE OWEN*		
PART NO.	SHIFT			
	1	2	3	TOTAL
230	*115*			*115*
274	*300*			*300*

Fig. 7–12 Scrap report prepared by quality control department and forwarded to the foreman.

Overtime Report. Particular care must be taken by the foreman to accumulate and report hours worked by any employee beyond the normal eight-hour shift. The overtime report should specify why overtime was required and should describe the skills used beyond the regular shift. This kind of information is needed so that the details peculiar to a given operation or department can be documented. With proper documentation predetermined overtime can be provided for when future budgets are prepared.

When a foreman relies upon overtime, he must also accept the fact that its use causes deterioration in departmental performance. If overtime is necessary because of cyclic activities or for other unusual recurring conditions, then it should be recognized and incorporated into the normal budget.

Equipment Performance Report. It is desirable to report any unusual circumstance related to machinery and equipment. It is especially important to report any problem that seems to require maintenance or repair, or which might lead to downtime.

The foreman is generally responsible for requesting that repair work be initiated. He should also follow up to be sure that the work is actually accomplished and that the production equipment is back in running condition.

The foreman's report to higher management can take the form of a log or diary of actions taken. The following is an example:

1) Advised the maintenance department—maintenance department rebraced the machine. Feeds and speeds were then increased to authorized limits.
2) The automatic chip drag was down for periodic maintenance check-up.
3) It was found that locating pin had been scored resulting in the blank locating 1/4 in. beyond the proper position. Maintenance was immediately advised. As a result the pin was welded and blanks located properly.

BUDGETING

A budget at its best is a means of measuring and comparing operating expenses. The final responsibility for its success or failure is the direct responsibility of operating management. In developing a budget as a management tool, costs are isolated and responsibility assigned so that management can pinpoint where costs are out of line, and determine exactly who is responsible for this condition. Personalities are thus divorced from problems.

A budget is a projected plan of action for a period of time covering all aspects of a company. A budget is developed for each individual department and all the departmental budgets are then consolidated into a master budget for the total company. The foreman plays a vital role in the formulation of his budget and should be alert to see that planned expense items are properly justified and incorporated into the final budget. The company-wide budget developed from the budgets prepared for each department makes it possible to direct, coordinate, and integrate all operations into the company's activities and achieve the desired results.

Table VII-2. Plant-wide Budget for Manufacturing 100,000 Units.

| | Breakdown—Annual Budget | | | |
Expense Category	Budgeted Amount	Total Direct Labor	Total In-direct Labor	Total Manufac-turing Expense
Direct Labor				
Total Units to Be Produced × Standard	200,000			
Hours × Wage Rate		200,000		
Indirect Labor				
Indirect Salaries and Wages	88,000			
Fringe Benefits—Indirect	23,700			
Total Indirect Labor Incurred	111,700			
Total Net Indirect Labor			111,700	
Other Manufacturing Expense				
Maintenance Material	95,300			
Tool & Equipment Matl.	105,000			
Losses and Defects	15,400			
Fuel	—			
	46,000			
Fixed Expense	353,000			
Utilities	89,100			
Miscellaneous Other	2,900			
Total Other Mfg. Exp. Incurred	706,700			
Assessments	325,700			
Total Net Other Manufacturing Expense	1,032,400			1,032,400
TOTAL ANNUAL BUDGET				1,344,100

Shown in Table VII-2 is a pre-established budget for a plant to produce 100,000 units. This budget indicates the indirect labor and other expenses associated with the total plant operation.

Type of Budgets

All budgets may be classified as either fixed or flexible. The fixed budget is a complete operating plan for the budgeting period. Once this type of budget has been prepared, it is not subject to change during the budgeting period. Fixed budgets are generally used only by companies that are able to forecast with a high degree of accuracy because the product they manufacture and sell is not subject to sharp or sudden changes in demand.

The flexible budget, on the other hand, is developed with the expectation that sales, costs, and expenses may vary over the budgeting period. Companies whose products are

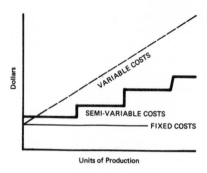

Fig. 7-13 Graphic   representation   of
fixed, semi-variable, and variable manufacturing costs.

subject to changes in demand are likely to find this type of budget both necessary and useful. Typical products for which this type of budgeting is desirable include those which are seasonal or cyclical in nature, those which are at the mercy of style changes (women's clothing, for example), or which are custom ordered. A flexible budget permits operating management to take account of factors that were not foreseen in their original planning and recognized changes in timing that may have occurred since the original budget was prepared. It also allows management to adjust for changes in economic conditions.

Types of Costs

Manufacturing costs can be classified as fixed, variable, or semi-variable. These cost patterns are shown in Fig. 7-13.

Fixed costs are those that remain the same regardless of production volume. Although they may change over relatively long periods, they are unaffected by short-term increases or decreases in the number of units produced. Examples include foremen's salaries, real estate taxes, rent, depreciation, and insurance.

Variable costs rise in direct proportion to the number of units produced. Direct costs such as material, labor, and perishable tooling (cutting tools, for example) usually follow a variable curve such as the one shown in Fig. 7-13.

Semi-variable costs are those that remain stable over a given number of production units but which jump sharply at certain incremental changes in volume. The cost of a machine capable of producing 50 units a day, for example, would be the same whether 10 or 50 units were manufactured. At 51 units, however, a new machine would have to be purchased, thus doubling the cost of machinery.

Budgetary Controls

A system of budgetary control is necessary for the development and effective use of a company-wide budget. Through proper budgetary controls appropriate input information is obtained from foremen and other supervisors in order to compile the overall budget. Proper controls are also essential to ensure continuing compliance with the budget. The standard cost system discussed earlier in this chapter, with its emphasis on variances from preestablished standards is one such method of control.

By means of budgetary controls the foreman's reports of actual performance are continually compared with objectives. When unfavorable variances are found, corrective action is taken to bring actual performance in line with budgeted cost goals.

Budgetary control performs a function similar to that of a fire or burglar alarm system. Nothing happens as long as the situation is under control, but the moment costs begin rising excessively variances sound the alarm to take action.

Reporting of Deviations

Budgets are developed to chart the course, to analyze current performance in relation to company goals, and to isolate the cause or reason for deviations. It is important to determine what can be done about a budget deviation and to properly fix the responsibility for correction.

Recognition of deviation to plan is a vital tool of budgeting. No budget is perfect, rather the budget serves as a yardstick; it is based on human judgment and is subject to error. Furthermore, it can be changed when new information becomes available.

If management is notified promptly that something is wrong, that a deviation has occurred, for example, action can be taken earlier and is usually less expensive. Deviation to plan allows management to perform inspection of the weak points in the budget and take the necessary action for correction.

The supervisor therefore should report immediately any deviations and indicate to management the weak areas requiring help.

SUMMARY

This chapter has tried to point out the responsibilities that foremen have in regard to costs. Only by being aware of his cost control responsibilities can the foreman aid in keeping manufacturing costs at a minimum. Important areas in which the foreman should monitor and control his costs are direct labor, machine utilization, scrap, rework, and material usage.

The standard cost system and departmental budgets are two tools designed to assist the foreman in meeting his cost control responsibilities. By reporting accurately his department's performance, the foreman can assure that accurate standard costs are established and unfavorable variances detected. By participating in the budget preparation process, the foreman can help in developing both departmental and company-wide budgets that will aid in cost control rather than hindering the cost control effort.

Chapter 8

The Foreman and
the Future

Earlier chapters have examined the foreman's responsibilities in some detail. Suggestions have been made to assist the first-line supervisor in attaining company objectives through participative leadership and other techniques, tactics, and strategies. This chapter examines the role of the foreman as that role exists today and as it may exist tomorrow and on into the more distant future. It is emphasized that the foreman or first-line manager must learn to evaluate his own performance in terms of past and present practice. Beyond this, however, the foreman should attempt to assess his capacity to meet future requirements and challenges.

THE PAST

Throughout business and industry there is a growing realization of the importance of evaluating ones past and present performance. The foreman's job involves planning, directing, and coordinating other people's activities. His ability to do this depends on how much he knows about himself and his relations with the people with whom he deals. The past is the great storehouse of experience, and from it past generations have derived many of the laws and principles that guide our society today. The present bears the imprint of what occurred earlier, and thus we are wise to turn to the past. To do this, daily records are necessary so that the first line supervisor can know from day to day how he is doing and what he has done.

The supervisor has learned by seeing things happen. His knowledge has been made up by a series of disconnected facts. Usually, he has not been in an environment where it has been customary to use a scientific method of keeping accurate records of his past experience. Foremen should be encouraged to record various happenings so they can be studied in their relationship to one another. General principles must be developed from particular instances well thought out.

A supervisor who is truly a manager must be a thinking and responsible person. His day's activities call for thoughtful reflection. He must review what seemed to be disconnected experiences and determine the common themes that apply. He must evaluate his own productivity and determine why he did or did not do what he knew he should have done. He may find that he is prone to delay or procrastination.

Procrastination is usually thought of as putting off until tomorrow what should be done today. The word implies an inexcusable delay such as that caused by indifference or through laziness. It is often said, "The busy people get things done." Likewise it is also said that, "The less one has to do, the less time one has to do it in." Here we see two habit patterns where some are activists while others:

1) Invent pretexts for doing something else
2) Picture the future with great fondness as full of all the time needed to get things done
3) Have the natural desire to escape thinking during the present
4) Don't have the energy to do a job now
5) Vacillate and end up doing nothing
6) Avoid unpleasant tasks
7) Require an extra push to do something out of the ordinary right now
8) Overestimate themselves and try to do five tasks in the time allotted to one, and when they can't keep up, they just skip the whole five instead of doing one properly.

Those who customarily procrastinate do so for several reasons:

1) *Laziness.* The first big reason is sheer laziness. Laziness can become a habit. We put off the thing that takes a lot of effort. We *mean* to get it done some day—we really do. But today we just don't have the energy. And tomorrow? Better to buckle down *now* and get it over with!
2) *Indecision.* When we have to make decisions about small, unimportant matters, we may vacillate for such a long time that we end up doing nothing.
3) *Avoiding unpleasant tasks.* Funny how we don't procrastinate with the things we enjoy doing; it's the ones we'd like to shirk that we put off.
4) *Looking through the wrong end of the spyglass.* We're busy all the time—so busy that we're busy with busyness part of the time. Stopping a minute to realize what the really important things are will make you concentrate on ensuring them first.
5) *Unreasonable fear.* One might fear, for example, that chest pain means heart trouble. Then again, it might not. But we're afraid of what the doctor might tell us. So, childishly, we don't go to the doctor.
6) *Inability to break routine.* Once we settle into a pattern of habitual action, it takes a little extra push to do something out of the ordinary—to visit the doctor or take the night-school course.
7) *Overestimating ourselves.* We can overestimate ourselves and our time and energy. We expect to be able to do five chores in the time allotted to one, and when we can't keep up, we just skip the whole five instead of doing one properly.

We don't *have* to procrastinate. Whatever the cause, procrastination is really just a bad habit. It takes a lot of effort, but habits can be changed. Any habit that costs us this much time, trouble and effort *should* be changed. Here are some suggestions that might help:

1) The first step in eliminating procrastination is to recognize that you *are* procrastinating. Once you face that fact, you can be on your guard against it.

2) Make a plan. An old business slogan is: "Plan your work and work your plan." If you do these two in rapid succession you can eliminate the tendency to put things off. Why not plan your day the night before so you can begin the day by *acting?* Try giving yourself deadlines—they might help.

3) "Once begun, is half done!" You'll never get far with anything unless you start. The first sentence of a letter is the hardest. Once you get into a task, you are more apt to carry it through. But if you don't make a beginning, you'll never be able to write "finished" to anything.

4) Tackle the difficult or unpleasant jobs first and get them out of the way. Save the easy things and the ones you enjoy doing for the last. Take a tip from the youngster who always saves his favorite food till last.

5) Analyze the things that mean most to you and your family: health, safety, security—and put these at the top of your list of things to be attended to.

6) Don't kid yourself. Don't promise yourself the unattainable or attempt the job you know you can't do. Good intentions must be tempered with realism about your own limitations in both time and energy.

7) Don't waste time making a big decision about a trivial matter. Unimportant things should be decided on quickly. If you wear yourself out on trivia, you're bound to neglect the important things.

8) Force yourself to step out of your everyday routine. Do it until you've built a new habit. Then when you have to do it, it will come easy to you.

9) Write down, right now, the things you must not put off any longer. Go over your list again next week and see how many items you can check off.[1]

Bernard Haldane wrote a book which counters the philosophy "profit from your mistakes."[2] Instead, he advocates that a person study his past *achievements* and those qualities and capabilities that made the achievements possible. An achievement is something which gives an individual a feeling of pride. It stirs emotions and gives a person a lift. It is an experience he would like to repeat frequently—in fact, the oftener the better.

THE PRESENT

The past is gone, and the future is yet to come. It is in the present that we live our lives and it is the present that must be changed if the future is to be different.

It is habits engaged in the present that are important. The foreman who wishes to be effective, who will influence his and his company's future:

1) Puts all his effort and ability into the solution of problems assigned him
2) Looks for work when he has free time
3) Often does something extra
4) Takes work home with him when necessary
5) Takes advantage of opportunities to show initiative
6) Takes pride in the work he does

---

1. Reed, Dena Pamphlet, *Procrastination—Are You Guilty.* Birk & Company. (New York, N.Y.).
2. Bernard Haldane, "How to Make a Habit of Success." *Readers Digest* (July, 1961). Prentice-Hall, Inc. (Englewood Cliffs, N.J., 1960).

7) Goes ahead on his own
8) Is easily stimulated to work on a problem
9) Has a real interest in his job
10) Strives to do better and better
11) Accepts an unusual assignment as a broadening experience
12) Has more than a casual interest in his work
13) Makes small self-improvements from time to time
14) Tries to overcome his limitations
15) Works to improve his weaknesses.[3]

William J. Reilly has written a book describing what he calls "the law of intelligent action."[4] This law should help the foreman who wishes to understand his own behavior. Reilly defines intelligent action as follows: "A person can be said to act intelligently in any given environment whenever he satisfactorily solves the problems of that environment."

In its simplest terms, Reilly expresses the law of intelligent action as follows:

When a person is confronted with a problem, the intelligence of his action is dependent on three primary factors:
1. His DESIRE to solve the problem.
2. His ABILITY to solve it.
3. His CAPACITY for handling the human relations involved.

Desire

We must be genuinely interested in a problem to achieve success in solving it. We must really desire to be in the environment. To evaluate himself in relation to his environment, the foreman should ask two questions:

1) Is it something that I really want to do?
2) Is it something that I believe in doing?

Ability

If the foreman can answer the above two questions in a positive manner, then he must ask himself whether or not he has the ability to solve the problems that he faces in this environment. If he feels somewhat inadequate, then he must make a sincere effort to develop or improve his abilities. In some cases, while he is improving his abilities he may be able to seek staff help from industrial engineers, production control, etc. He should make use of services available from the staff. He should upgrade and update himself through all the available means possible: machine and equipment manufacturers' assistance, magazines, technical societies, and in-plant and outside adult education courses, for example.

Capacity

The capacity for handling the human relations involved is very important. A man can be very competent technically but may be lacking in his capacity for getting along with

---

3. John C. South, "Human Motivation and Continuing Engineering Studies," *Journal of Engineering Education* Vol. 56, No. 5 (January, 1966), 166–67.

4. William J. Reilly, *The Law of Intelligent Action* (Harper & Brothers, 1945), 13 and 17.

people. Our understanding and judgment of others largely determines whether we are headed for success or are destined for failure and disappointment. Too few use the "intelligent selfishness" approach of talking and thinking in terms of others rather than talking and thinking in terms of himself. The intelligent selfishness approach is founded upon the Golden Rule: "Do for others as you would have them to do for you."

IMMEDIATE FUTURE

As already indicated our future expectations depend upon our present behavior. Our present behavior requires that we have a single and intense purpose.

The future is now. High producing first-line managers do not neglect the tools and resources provided by scientific management. They attack their problems with determination. They use new measurement tools; they abandon old outmoded theories. As Likert stresses in his book, *The Human Organization,* they use these quantitative tools in special ways—ways that achieve significantly higher motivation than is obtained by those first-line managers who adhere strictly to methods specified by the traditional theory of management. A central concept of the modified theory is:

1) That the pattern of interaction between the first-line manager and those with whom he deals should always be such that the individuals involved will feel that the manager is dealing with them in a *supportive* rather than a *threatening* manner.

2) That management will make full use of the *potential* capacities *of its human resources only* when each person in an organization is a member of a *well-knit and effectively functioning work group* with high interaction skills and performance goals.[5]

High producing first-line managers are interested in these tools that achieve significantly higher motivation and performance. They are interested in:

1) Knowing what activities take the most time
2) Pinpointing misdirected effort
3) Ascertaining that skills are being used properly
4) Determining if employees are performing too many unrelated tasks
5) Finding out if tasks are spread too thinly
6) Making sure that work is distributed evenly
7) Verifying whether or not time is being spent on essential work
8) Feedback of the "score of the game."

Motivation—Give People the Score

To experiment with this philosophy of scorekeeping, Wolf[6] in the paper industry in 1918 decided that he should make the operators of the machinery conscious participators in the entire process of production. He recognized each operator as a manager of his own area. Therefore, he made it a point to supply to each operator, on a daily basis, records

---

5. Rensis Likert, *The Human Organization: Its Management and Value* (McGraw-Hill: New York, 1967).
6. Robert B. Wolf, "Management Engineering in the Paper Industry—The Measurement of Performance a Factor in Good Management—Industry Should be Organized to Encourage Rather than Repress Individual Development," *Mechanical Engineering* (May, 1923), 295.

showing product cost, quality, and volume variations. He gave them the score of the game. Today, we call this responsibility accounting.

These records were developed in direct cooperation with the men. It was significant that their sympathetic interest in the work came from a realization that it meant *greater opportunity to use their brain power with more chance for individual development.*

Work measurement must be a cooperative effort. This program must meet the needs of the personnel being served. The score of the game must always be presented rapidly to the employees.

Imagine what football would be like if the game score were not fed back to the spectators and the players themselves. The magic ingredient of football, baseball, or any other game is score keeping. This is feedback in its most familiar form. It is prompt, accurate, easily understood, and universally reported. In other words, the score is fed back not just to the front office, but to every player and spectator.

Yet in industry men and women are often asked to work eight hours a day, week after week, and millions of them are never given any "score" as to how they are doing their work. Is it any wonder that these employees are not interested in their work?

Appley tells about an attitude survey conducted in a large company:

> The oustanding desire most generally expressed by the individuals questioned was for more details and accurate knowledge on one particular subject: "How am I doing?" . . . if the extent to which individuals are kept informed of their progress and the skill with which this is done would be tripled in every organization in the next twelve months, the resulting impact upon company performance, or economy and society in general would be almost beyond comprehension.[7]

Performance feedback is an approach which results in a hard-hitting information system showing the "score of the game."

An integrated report system gives the first-line manager the answer to that question: "How am I doing?" Likewise, the information, if deemed necessary, can be collected on an individual basis to answer this same question. The foreman must be held responsible; he must be concerned about overall departmental performance; and in turn he must relate this activity to the individual attainment of goals.

Goal Setting

It is not failure, but low aim which is worthy of criticism. It is the man of concentration who cuts his way through obstacles and achieves success. A foreman who knows where he is going and directs his efforts properly toward carrying out his objectives is bound to progress. It is evident that setting a goal is of primary importance. Goals are the starting points of thought and action. The requirements of achieving a goal should be specified with respect to quantity, quality, time, and cost. The foreman must be willing to sacrifice and expend effort to meet his goal. His goal should fit into the overall business organization of which he is a part.

A business is primarily an economic institution. Its primary objectives are related to acquiring, creating, preserving, or distributing goods or services. Achievement of business objectives depends upon the satisfactory integration of personal objectives with organizational objectives.

Appraisal of results depends upon constant feedback. This feedback was given the name cybernetics by Norbert Wiener. The new science of cybernetics has furnished us

---

7. Lawrence A. Appley, "The Present Scratchpad," *Management News,* American Management Assoc. (November, 1954), 1.

with convincing proof that the subconscious mind is not a mind at all, but a mechanism—a goal-striving "servo-mechanism" consisting of the brain and the nervous system which is used by and directed by the mind. Our brains are much more complex than any electronic brain or guided missile ever conceived by man. Our system works automatically to achieve goals of success. The word "cybernetics" comes from a Greek word which means literally "the steersman." Servo-mechanisms are constructed so that they automatically steer their way to a target. Maxwell Maltz chose to call the new concept (where we conceive of the human brain and nervous system as a form of servo-mechanism) "psycho-cybernetics."[8] This term is used to emphasize the principles of cybernetics as applied to the human brain. The concept is not that man is a machine but rather that he has a mechanism which he uses, which acts very similar to a servo-mechanism.

Maltz explains the concept by citing the squirrel as an example. A squirrel born in the spring, Maltz points out, has never experienced winter. Yet in the fall of the year, he can be observed busily storing nuts to be eaten during the winter months when there will be no food to be gathered. The squirrel does not have to be taught how to gather food, nor does it have to be taught the necessity of storing food for winter.

Man on the other hand, has something animals don't have, creative imagination. Man is more than a creature, he is a creator. With his imagination he can formulate a variety of goals. Man alone can direct his success mechanism by the use of imagination. We often think of "creative imagination" as applying only to poets, inventors, and the like. But creative imagination can apply to everyone.

Servo-mechanisms are capable of solving two types of problems: (1) problems where the target, goal, or "answer" is known and the purpose is to reach it and (2) problems where the target or "answer" is not known and the objective is to discover or locate it. The human brain and nervous system can operate to solve either type of problem.

An example of the first step is the self-guided torpedo, or interceptor missile. The target or goal is known—an enemy ship or plane. The objective is to reach it. A torpedo must "know" the target it is aimed at. It must have some sort of propulsion system which pushes it forward in the general direction of the target. It must be equipped with a "sense organ" (radar, sonar, heat perceptors, etc.) which brings information from the target. These "sense organs" inform the missile that it is on the correct course (positive feedback) or that it has committed an error and gone off course (negative feedback). The torpedo does not respond to positive feedback; it is doing the correct thing already and simply continues "doing what it is doing." There must be a corrective device, however, which will respond to negative feedback. When negative feedback informs the missile that it is "off the beam" too far to the right, the corrective mechanism automatically causes the rudder to move so that it will steer the torpedo back to the left. If it "overcorrects" and heads too far to the left, this mistake is made known through negative feedback and the corrective device moves the rudder so that it will steer the missile back to the right. The torpedo accomplishes its goal by going forward, making errors, and continually correcting them. By a series of zigzags it literally "gropes" its way to the goal.

This example illustrates how timely feedback can enable the foreman to stay on course. By knowing at all times whether his actions are in keeping with the objectives at which they are directed, the foreman also knows whether to continue doing what he has done in the past or whether to make changes. A series of small corrective changes will

---

8. Maxwell Maltz, *Psyco-Cybernetics, A New Way to Get More Living Out of Life* (Prentice-Hall, Inc., 1960).

ensure that his actions remain goal directed, and the chances of attaining overall company goals and objectives are enhanced.

The Vital Few—The Trivial Many

A system of priorities provides us with a guide indicating which activities or items come first. We have all heard the statement, "Do first things first." Charles Schwab, president of Bethlehem Steel during the World War I period, once learned a lesson concerning the establishment of priorities that is well worth repeating:

One day, years ago, efficiency expert Ivy Lee was interviewing Charles Schwab, president of Bethlehem Steel Company. Lee outlined his organization's service, by concluding, "With our service you will know how to manage better."

"Well," said Schwab, "I'm not managing as well now as I know how to. We don't need more 'knowing' but more 'doing.' If you can give us something to pep us up to do the things we already know we ought to do, I will gladly listen to you and pay you anything within reason you ask."

"Fine," answered Lee, "I can give you something in 20 minutes that will step up your doing at least 50 percent."

"Okay," said Schwab. "Let's have it! I have just about that much time before I have to catch a train."

Lee handed Schwab a blank sheet of notepaper and said: "Write down the six most important tasks you have to do tomorrow and number them in the order of their importance. Now, put this paper in your pocket and the first thing tomorrow morning look at item one and start working on it until it is finished. Then tackle item two in the same way; then item three, and so on. Do this until quitting time. Do not be concerned if you have only finished one or two. You will be working on the most important ones. The others can wait. If you cannot finish them all by this method, you could not have with any other method, and without some system, you would probably not even have decided which was the most important.

"Do this every working day. After you have convinced yourself of the value of this system, have your men try it. Try it as long as you wish, and then send me a check for whatever you think it is worth."

In a few weeks, Schwab sent Lee a check for $25,000 with a letter saying the lesson was the most profitable he had ever learned. In five years, this plan was largely responsible for turning the unknown Bethlehem Steel Company into the biggest independent steel producer in the world.

If this lesson was so valuable to Schwab, why shouldn't we use it to better utilize our time and multiply our efforts?

In recording and analyzing current behavior, Pareto's Law can be applied. Pareto's Law has been applied in inventory control. Inventory items are arranged in a frequency distribution with the number one item being that which involves the most cost, the number two item the one involving the second highest cost, the number three item involving the third highest cost, etc.

Inventory items are arranged on a graph (see Fig. 8-1) so that the dollar value of the inventory on the Y axis represents 100 percent and all of the number of items on the X axis represents 100 percent. The curve then can be divided into approximately the following percentages. Five percent of the most costly items which we shall call "A" items represents 60% of the dollar value, and 25% of the most costly items represents 85% of the dollar value. This next 20% (between 5% and 25%) we shall call "B" items and the

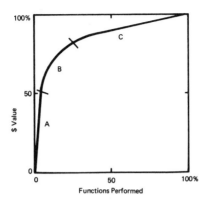

Fig. 8-1 Graph utilizing Pareto's curve to indicate quantity and value of inventory items.

remaining 75% "C" items. Obviously, this arrangement requires that "A" items be controlled more closely than "B" items and "C" items require the least control.

On the Pareto or ABC curve we could substitute the functions we perform in our work on the X axis and dollar value of these functions on the Y axis. Thus we are evaluating performance of our activities in terms of their value to us and to the industry, or business we are serving. This provides a means of looking at our tasks in terms of doing "first things first." Joseph Juran, an authority in industrial engineering, expressed this concept as a way to review the "vital few" activities and the "trivial many."

Don Schoeller, in a talk before the American Institute of Industrial Engineers[9] in 1965, emphasized the need for a Time Utilization Log to help ascertain how management is employing time (see Fig. 8-2). As a part of this logging process he recommended that individuals place their activities in A, B, C priority. He also recommended that a self-study device be used called an "Exectutrol" which uses a ten-channel tape to record the time spent by a manager on a specific task on a given work day. This portable device actually forces the manager to become his own time study man. This enables him to determine how he distributes his activities in terms of concentration on key result areas. To log or record activities the following procedure is used:

First take a blank sheet of paper and write down everything you *should* be doing for the next three weeks, three months, or whatever period of time you think will cover at least a representative sample of the total tasks for which you are held accountable. Your job description, if you have one, may provide you with some clues as to what you should be doing.

When you have most of them down, number them, not according to when they have to be done, but according to what *return or "value" the item* has to the enterprise. (It is always good to check with your boss at this stage if you can.)

Take the top 15 percent of your items and label these *A* items, the next 20 percent *B* items, and the other 65 percent and label them *C* items. Then take this list and lock it away in your desk drawer.

9. V. Donald Schoeller, "The Industrial Engineer and Management Performance Standards," *Sixteenth Annual Conference and Convention Proceedings* (May 13-15, 1965), 263-276.

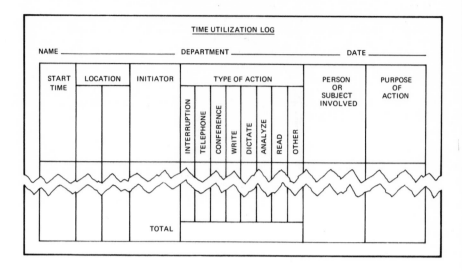

Fig. 8–2   Time utilization log.

Second, make some copies of the Time Utilization Log. Starting as soon as you can, keep a record of everything you do. Put this form on top of your desk, and carry it with you when you go somewhere. Put it in your briefcase when you travel. Log your time.

Third, analyze, using the check lists and the following ideas:

1) To determine which activities come first, we have to relate everything to the purpose of the function. Define your purpose. Who does it? Can disagreement as to purpose create difficulties in deciding which things to do first? When this happens, who should settle the issue?

2) Even after we have decided which things come first, the problem of relative importance has not been settled. The principle of "first things first" can revolutionize our approach to time, to delegation, and to appraisal of our total effectiveness.

3) Job pressure and other kinds of stress influence the choices we make. When overworked, we are more likely to direct our attention to items of lesser importance because they make us feel more comfortable.

How can we solve this problem? At best, each of us compromise. Yet, as we become more *aware* of what we are doing, and have more precise tools for measuring significance, we discover new meanings for "obvious" happenings.

It does little good to talk about such matters. Talk alone rarely helps one learn how to apply new approaches. Therefore, this "assignment" will give you experience with actions implementing the new approaches.

Remember that this is not an analysis to be collected or turned over to any outside expert. The *expert* in this case is you. The person who knows your activity best is *you.* Through self-analysis, you will benefit from an "energy jump." You will increase your personal effectiveness as an individual and as a manager.

Fourth, take some action! Get rid of *C* or *B* items! Delegate. Concentrate on the *A* items.

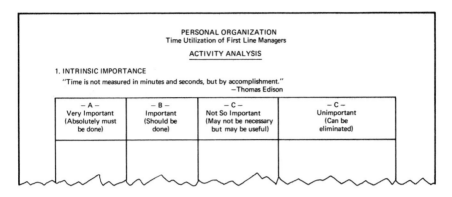

Fig. 8-3   Activity analysis—intrinsic importance.

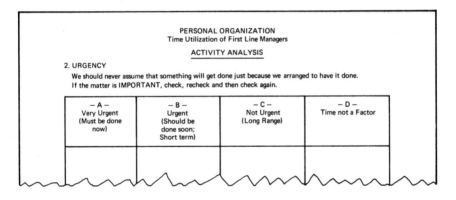

Fig. 8-4   Activity analysis—urgency.

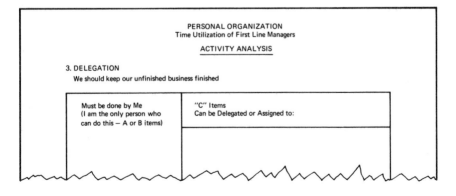

Fig. 8-5   Activity analysis—delegation.

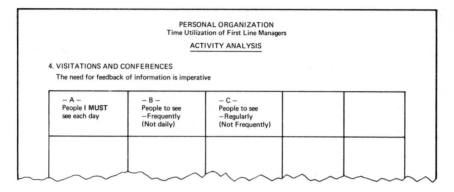

Fig. 8–6   Activity analysis—visitations and conferences.

Fifth, complete your first round of analysis and make improvements where possible. Then, take out the list, review it with your boss and your subordinates, set new goals and objectives, and make a new list. You are now on your way to a continual personal improvement program.

To fully analyze the importance of various activities the first-line manager may use the activity analysis charts made up into four categories:

1) Activity analysis—intrinsic importance (Fig. 8-3)
2) Activity analysis—urgency (Fig. 8-4)
3) Activity analysis—delegation (Fig. 8-5)
4) Activity analysis—visitations and conferences (Fig. 8-6)

LONG-RANGE FUTURE

Today's objectives can become reality provided we establish and carry out specific plans to accomplish them. An objective is an image in the mind of the foreman of what he hopes to accomplish. This image can become real to the extent he is willing to apply himself. New Year's resolutions are often laughed at because they are so frequently broken. Objectives are just as easily discarded unless there is a primary and overriding objective to continuously review established goals and work toward their accomplishment.

To attain objectives, standards of measurement are needed. People want to "know the score." Foremen must motivate themselves continuously to do a better job. The performance of a foreman is reflected by the performance of his people. He must have sufficient knowledge of each employees' job to recognize when good results occur. Likewise, he must take a corrective action when poor results are called to his attention.

Furthermore, to achieve outstanding performance from subordinates, foremen should set examples of outstanding performance themselves. For many years the function of industrial engineers has been to set engineered work measurement standards for hourly rated personnel. Standards of performance for foremen are of necessity less exact because the foreman's work is more judgmental in nature. These standards are usually set by means of a conference between the foreman and his superior. Even in the foreman's job, however, many things can be measured.

These standards are usually preceded by a very complete position description of the foreman's job. Then each statement of the position description is recorded in the performance standard with a subsequent statement, "This function is up to standard when . . ." (a satisfactory goal is attained).

Satisfactory goals should be based on satisfactory past performance. They should require normal results attainable by men of average capabilities. The standards should be as specific as possible. Time, percentages, specified cost reductions, and explicit quality and quantity figures or ratios should be defined in detail. Sometimes a check list may aid in bringing about this clear-cut detailed analysis of a job well done. By following this kind of performance measurement a foreman knows, himself, even before he is evaluated by his superior whether or not he is doing a good job. This performance measurement approach helps answer the question that everyone wants answered, "How am I doing?"

Raymond F. Valetine, head of the Performance Review Section, U.S. Naval Aviation Supply Office, Philadelphia, prepared a record for the American Management Association in which he specifically stressed the understanding of performance objectives which he defines as follows:

> A performance objective is a statement describing the conditions that will exist when a key area of a job is being done well. Included in the statement is a yardstick or measure which spells out the degree of achievement. An example of an objective is "Maintain rejections at less than 2% of total units produced." In this instance, the key area being covered is production which meets specifications or quality standards. The yardstick is percentage of rejections. The condition which indicates that the job is being done well is that rejections are less than 2% of total units produced.
>
> Setting the target at a very precise point is not necessary. It is of much greater importance that the objectives call for future performance at a level higher than is currently being achieved, that they incorporate practical yardsticks, and that they be clearly understood by both the manager and his boss.
>
> It is especially advantageous to set an objective at a point which requires a high level of performance. If the manager must stretch his skills and efforts to achieve the yardstick, some of his latent ability will be developed in the process. Here we have a practical example of the inherent usefulness of targets. The conscious act of setting a high objective and keeping it in the forefront virtually guarantees improved performance.
>
> Essential in developing statements of objectives is that each one should have a clear and understandable connection with company goals. The more direct the connection, the greater the stimulus for performance of true excellence. Objectives which include yardsticks stated in terms of costs, savings, profits, sales, and the like are particularly suitable, because they are significant and observable at both managerial and corporate levels. The manager who knows that the results he achieves will be seen by top management has plenty of motivation.[10]

Objectives are set jointly by the manager and his boss. This is the key to developing targets which are acceptable and meaningful. The manager's participation in setting his own goals is the essence of the communication process; it is fundamental to building the superior-subordinate relationship; it is the practical means for raising managerial motivation to a higher level. If the manager does not participate to a significant degree in setting his objectives, the major benefits which can be derived from them will be seriously diminished.

Furthermore, the performance measurement procedure followed by a regularly scheduled evaluation of progress between the foreman and his superior assures that objectives are stressed in the minds of both. The likelihood that these objectives will be

10. Raymond F. Valentine, "The Goal-Setting Session." 12-inch, 33-1/3 rpm microgroove recording. monoral (American Management Association, 1967).

finalized is increased. The planned follow-up compels action and vitalized goals that might otherwise deteriorate. Also, as changes occur, goals can be altered to make provision for unexpected developments.

NEW CONCEPTS OF SUPERVISION

Few aspects of human performance have greater interest or significance than the answer to the question, "How do I get what I want?" Numerous books have been written relating to the general principles of success, and the literature, fiction as well as non-fiction, is filled with examples of men who have risen from humble beginnings to achieve great success in life by applying the right principles and by being properly motivated. An early twentieth-century author, Orison Swett Marden, begins his book, *How to Get What You Want,* with the following statement:

> We establish relations with our desires, with whatever is dominant in our minds, for the things we long for with all our hearts, and we tend to realize these things in proportion to the persistency and intensity of our longings and our intelligent efforts ro realize them.[11]

John C. South defines motivation as the expenditure of physical and/or psychological energy directed toward a goal, object, or outcome which bears a distinct relationship to the nature of the energy. He continues to emphasize that attitudes, needs, interests, values, desires, and drives have sometimes been used interchangeably with motivation or under the heading of motivation. Human motivation is very complex; defined quite simply, however, it is that *something* that makes people proceed to higher and higher performance.

The most successful motivational programs have been those where the company has worked very closely with the individual's own personal objectives and goals.

In order to combat obsolescence of technical knowledge and skills and to update first-line management, the following conclusions have developed:

1) Provide in-service training
2) Sponsor education for employees at company expense
3) Encourage first-line managers to attend professional meetings at company expense
4) Provide for rotation of assignments
5) Develop seminars for foremen
6) Sponsor special professional society and/or university programs on specific phases of technical development.

We must "lift ourselves by our bootstraps." Because of technological change, we have to continuously change our customs which may require that we set up a long-term program of study. We must recognize that what we do in the way of adapting ourselves to further education and experience must come out of our own budget of leisure time.

Elimination of First-Line and Middle Management

Thousands of production systems, assembly lines, and industrial processes are now operated by numerically controlled or automated equipment programmed by computers

---

11. Orison Swett Marden, *How to Get What You Want* (Thomas Y. Crowell Company, 1917), 24.

or punched-tape instructions. Quality is improved, and the human factor is minimized. In the 1970s and 1980s, what is going to happen to first-line management and middle management? In the next thirty years it is expected that the computer will be programmed to run a factory in great detail. Changes with respect to organization structure will certainly occur. As first-line managers and as middle managers we must anticipate the future. What happens one year from now, ten years from now, and thirty years from now depends upon what we do today. We can only guess about the future. No one knows, with certainty, that we shall progress. On the other hand, we may even go into a state of regression. However, we tend toward the optimistic viewpoint. We must not overlook nor neglect planning the future as well as we can on the basis of present trends. A. W. Clausen, Executive Vice-President of the Bank of America, made the following statement:

> I disagree with the oft-expressed fear that the individual is in danger of becoming obsolete. I do not think there is any danger that the spinning tapes, blinking lights, and other products of electronic wizardry will ultimately run a world in which there is no more use for or need of man. . . . There is always a great deal of resistance to change and new concepts—usually from the people ensconced in a comfortable rut that is protected by the status quo. These people either do not want to, or are afraid to grow. And taken together they compose a powerful lobby for inertia in any corporation. When we allow this to happen, when we allow the drones to effectively rule the hive, the man who wants to grow and diversify hasn't a chance. And since he is the man the corporation needs to grow and diversify, this means the corporation hasn't got a chance either.[12]

Currently first-line managers are being encouraged to develop their sophistication and improve their education. As mechanization, automation, computerization, and electronic instrumentation continue to change the factory layout, it is imperative that the education level of first-line management rise. Greater record keeping will be required so that future operations can be controlled more meticulously. Future expectations depend upon past experiences. This experience must be accurately recorded so that improved decisions may be made. Even then decisions must contain provision for innovation, and in the final analysis they are dependent upon people. Therefore, first-line managers, the individuals directly responsible for producing the product, must always be in the picture regardless of how well we can pass on to a computer certain aspects of the decision-making process.

John M. Bergey and Robert C. Slomer, of the Hamilton Watch Company, presented an article, "Administration in the 1980's,"[13] in which they reviewed some of the possible trends of the future. In their research they conclude that, "It is possible to choose practically any approach to the future and find someone who will vehemently support this proposal." Nevertheless, after searching the literature they came up with the following points which represent their summary view of administration in the 1980s:

1) The future manager will be better grounded in social sciences, world affairs, and the humanities in general. He will be the catalyst that will effectively integrate the techniques of information technology with the human resources available to him.
2) Although the great majority of routine administrative functions will be computerized, the computer specialists will not constitute a new management elite.

12. A. W. Clausen, "Personal Growth in the World of Challenge," *SAM Advanced Management Journal* (October, 1969), 22.

13. John Bergey and Robert C. Slomer, "Administration in the 1980's," *SAM Advanced Management Journal* (April, 1969), 25–32.

3) Government will play an increasingly influential role in the business enterprise of the future. There will be a sense of mutual dependence between government and the business community as they will both work to solve the rampaging problems of society.

4) Universities will be the source of future managers as the management curriculum will be an accepted and formalized body of knowledge. Working up through the ranks will be a very unlikely path for the future professional manager.

5) Since the computer will perform most routine tasks presently performed by middle management, the manager of the future will devote much of his efforts to further the long range potential of his organization as it directly relates to the social environment of the times.

6) Since the social scientists will have learned much about using the computer to predict behavioral patterns, selection of future managers will necessarily become much more objective. Tradition, family ties, and seniority will disappear as a basis for selection of managers.

7) Organizational structures will become less pyramidal, nearly impossible to chart with present techniques, and more flexible in their ability to respond to a rapidly changing and fluid environment.

8) One of the prime responsibilities of the future managers will be planning. Top management will plan for longer time spans, perhaps 20 years, while the lowest levels will be concerned with only the next several years.

9) Though the profit motive will still be the driving force of business in the 1980s, the search for profit will be strongly affected by management awareness of the social consequences of their decisions.

Thus, the future of management will be judged by both its impact on society and its involvement with the new technology. There will be a kind of wholeness—not science apart, but science and technology as determinants of the human condition of the future. The future manager's influence will be greater, will affect more people, and will occur in a more fluid society than any time, past or present.

Machine Specialist versus People Specialist

The question arises as to how much human relations can be combined with technical training. Technology is advancing rapidly and there is much to learn with regard to electronics, numerical control, digital computers, closed circuit TV, micro-miniaturization, etc. Sandwiched in this whole program is the need to have an understanding of human relations. While there is an emphasis today upon broadening managers to be people as well as machine oriented, it appears that we will continue on the path toward greater specialization. In spite of this specialization, it will be imperative that the future first-line manager become better grounded in human relations.

CONCLUSION

We have seen great strides in manufacturing and management during the past one hundred years, and the future will see even greater improvements. In conclusion let us quote Orison Swett Marden, who wrote a book in 1894 entitled, *Pushing to the Front; or, Success Under Difficulties.* The author gives the objective of the book as follows:

The author's aim has been to spur the perplexed youth to act the Columbus to his own undiscovered possibilities; to urge him not to brood over the past . . . but to get his lesson from the hour; to encourage him to make every occasion a great occasion. . . . to show him that he must not wait for his opportunity, but make it.[14]

While some of us may not be young physically, we are all in a state of youth with respect to the potentialities of the future. The philosophy and the principles of utilizing the hour still prevails.

14. Orison Swett Marden, *Pushing to the Front; or, Success Under Difficulties* (The Riverside Press: Cambridge, Mass, 1894), Preface, iii.

Bibliography

Bass, Bernard M. and James A. Vaughan, *Training in Industry: Management of Learning.* Belmont, California: Wadsworth Publishing Company, 1970.

Bittle, Lester R., *What Every Supervisor Should Know,* 2nd ed. New York: McGraw-Hill Book Company, 1968.

Black, James M. and Guy B. Ford, *Front-Line Management.* New York: McGraw-Hill Book Company, 1963.

Carson, Gordon B., *Production Handbook,* 2nd ed. New York: The Ronald Press Company, 1959.

Cenci, Louis, *Skill Training for the Job.* New York: Pitman Publishing Corporation, 1966.

Corder, G. G., *Organizing Maintenance.* London, England: British Institute of Management, 1963.

Denova, Charles, *Establishing a Training Function: A Guide for Management.* Englewood Cliffs, New Jersey: Educational Technology Publications, Inc., 1970.

Dudick, T. S., *Cost Controls for Industry.* Englewood Cliffs, New Jersey: Prentice Hall, Inc., 1962.

Eilon, S., *Elements of Production Planning and Control.* New York: The Macmillan Company, 1962.

Eninger, M. U., *Accident Prevention Fundamentals for Managers and Supervisors.* Pittsburgh, Pennsylvania: Normax Publications, Inc., 1965.

Gellerman, S. W., *Motivation and Productivity.* New York: American Management Association, 1963.

Graham, C. F., *Work Measurement and Cost Control.* New York: Pergamon Press, Inc., 1965.

Grant, E., *Statistical Quality Control.* 3rd ed. New York: McGraw-Hill Book Company, 1964.

Haire, Mason, *Psychology in Management.* New York: McGraw-Hill Book Company, 1964.

Haseman, Wilbur C., *Managerial Uses of Accounting.* Boston: Allyn & Bacon, Inc., 1963.

Henrici, S. B., *Standard Costs for Manufacturing.* 3rd ed. New York: McGraw-Hill Book Company, Inc., 1960.

Herzberg, Frederick, *Work and the Nature of Man.* Cleveland, Ohio: World Publishing Company, 1966.

Ireson, W. G. (ed.), *Reliability Handbook.* New York: McGraw-Hill Book Company, 1966.

Juran, J. M. (ed.), *Quality Control Handbook.* New York: McGraw-Hill Book Company, 1962.

Kellogg, Marion S., *Closing the Performance Gap.* New York: Macmillan Company, 1967.

Magee, John F. and David M. Boodman, *Production Planning and Inventory Control.* 2nd ed. New York: McGraw-Hill Book Company, 1967.

Marting, Elizabeth (ed.), *AMA Book of Employment Forms.* New York: American Management Association, 1967.

McGarrah, Robert E., *Production and Logistics Management: Text and Cases.* New York: John Wiley & Sons, 1963.

McGregor, Douglas, *The Human Side of Enterprise.* New York: McGraw-Hill Book Company, 1960.

———, *The Professional Manager.* New York: McGraw-Hill Book Company, 1967.

Morrow, L. C., *Maintenance Engineering Handbook.* New York: McGraw-Hill Book Company, 1960.

Nadler, Gerald, *Work Design.* Homewood, Illinois: Richard D. Irwin, Inc. 1963.

Newbrough, E. T., *Effective Maintenance Management.* New York: McGraw-Hill Book Company, 1967.

Simons, R. H. and J. V. Grimaldi, *Safety Management.* Homewood, Illinois: Richard D. Irwin, 1956.

Staley, John D., *The Cost Minded Manager.* New York: The American Management Association, 1961.

Stokes, Paul M., *Total Job Training.* New York: American Management Association, 1966.

Vernon, Ivan R., (ed.), *Realistic Cost Estimating for Manufacturing.* Dearborn, Michigan: Society of Manufacturing Engineers, 1968.

Wolfbeing, Seymour, *Education and Training for Full Employment.* New York: Columbia University Press, 1967.

Zeyher, L. R., *Cost Reduction in the Plant.* Englewood Cliffs, New Jersey: Prentice Hall, Inc. 1966.

Index

Industrial relations, 33, 41–42
In-plant training
  employee, 65–67, 71–80
    learning principles, 72–73
    methods, 74–75
    minority worker, 78–79
    preparation for, 75–76
  foremen, 21–23 (*tables*)

L

Labor costs, 82–83
  reporting, 92–100
Labor relations, 41–42, 60–63
  disciplinary action, 61–63
  grievances, 61
Leadership, 17–18

M

Maintenance, 33, 47–49
  preventive, 88–89
Management styles, 52–54
  influential leadership, 53–54
  laissez-faire, 52–53
  taskmaster, 53
Manpower, 40–41
Manufacturing engineering, 12, 42–43
Material control, 33, 42
Material costs, 82–84
  reporting, 92–100
Middle management, 5, 33–34
Minority groups, 12–13
  training, 78–79
Motivation, 54–55, 109–110

O

Organization, 28–32
  specific, 31–32
  staffing, 28–31
Organizational theory, 25–28
  charts, 28–29
  theorist, 27
  theory X, 26–27
  theory Y, 27
  traditional, 25–26
Orientation, employee, 65–71

P

Pareto curve, 113
Personal characteristics, 17–18
Personnel department, 33, 38, 40–42, 66
Personnel relations, 15, 18–19
Plant engineering, 12, 48–49
Process engineering, 33, 45
Product engineering, 45

Production, 33, 34, 38, 42–44
Production control, 12
Production records, 47

Q

Quality control, 12, 33, 38–39, 44–46

R

Reports
  cost, 91–100
  disciplinary, 61–63
  orientation, 67–71

S

Safety, 49, 90
Scheduling, 43–44
Scrap and rework costs, 84–90
  reporting 98–100
Self-discipline, 105–107, 112–116
Self-improvement, 20, 21 (*table*), 22–24
Service groups, 33–34
Span of control, 32–33
Staffing, 28–31, 40–41
Standards, 44
Standards engineer, 44
Status, 19–20, 35
Superintendent (*see* General foreman)
Supervisor, 3
Supervisory skills, 5–6, 9, 17–18, 52–54
Systems, 38–50

T

Theory X, 26–27
Theory Y, 27
Timekeeping, 46–47
Time utilization, 113–116
Top management, 4–5, 33–34
Training, employee, 65–67, 71–80
  learning principles, 72–73
  methods, 74–75
  minority worker, 78–79
  preparation for, 75–76
Training, foreman, 20, 21 (*table*), 22–24, 44
Transportation, 33

W

Work habits, 17–18

V

Value analysis, 86–88

Z

Zero defects, 85–86